Parenting With Intimacy

— ■ —

EXPERIENCING GREAT COMMANDMENT LOVE IN YOUR FAMILY

Congratulations! You've made an important decision that will have far-reaching, even life-changing results. Considering all the other demands on your time, your willingness to tackle a workbook on parenting demonstrates that your family is important to you.

We realize that this will require an investment of your time which could otherwise be spent on other more personally pleasurable activities such as pursuing a favorite hobby, piloting through cyberspace, or perfecting your armchair quarter-backing skills. We promise to make it worth your while.

It's a decision you won't regret.

great commandment network

A global network empowering people to experience and reproduce great relationships through loving God and others

Parenting With Intimacy

David Ferguson
Paul Warren
Jim Walter
Terri Snead

All Scripture quotations, unless otherwise indicated, are taken from the Holy Bible, New International Version. Copyright 1973, 1978, 1984, by International Bible Society. Used by permission of Zondervan Publishing House. All rights reserved.

For more information contact:

The Great Commandment Network
2511 South Lakeline Blvd., Cedar Park, TX 78613
www.greatcommandment.net
800.881.8008
www.RelationshipPress.com

ISBN 0-9642845-9-6

Contents

Introduction:

Chapters:

Getting the Most
From This Workbook

This workbook is designed to be used by individuals, couples, and groups who want to learn how to make their family relationships more intimate, nurturing, and caring.

If you have picked up this workbook, you likely have a desire to see continued growth in your family relationships. You may even personally desire to learn how to have an intimate relationship with each of your children.

Each chapter contains practical ideas and thought-provoking exercises to help you develop a closer, more intimate relationship with your child or children. In addition to reading the text . . .

◆ You will be invited to **"Stop and consider"** something you've just read. You will have space to reflect and write your thoughts and feelings about important concepts and principles.

◆ You will be invited to specifically **"Apply the principles"** to your own children. You'll define how the principles could actually work in your own family relationships!

◆ Opportunities for **Scripture Reflection and Prayer** are found in several chapters which invite you to deepen your experience of God's love and care for you.

◆ Each chapter also contains an **"Experiencing Biblical Truth"** section where you will be guided to respond to and incorporate scriptural truth into your personal and family life. This is how lasting change occurs—as we experience Scripture, "being doers of the word!" (James 1:22).

◆ Finally, you will be given **"Homework For Your Home"**— assignments to help you develop and deepen "Great Commandment Love" as family lifestyle.

In addition, each chapter includes **"Special Thoughts for Single Parents"** and **"Special Thoughts for Blended Families."** We recognize the greater challenges and complexity of family life for all members of these families.

To get the most from this workbook, we urge you to do the following:

1. Set aside time each week to read the chapter and work through the "boxes" personally. All exercises are for individual work. Your personal preparation will prepare you for "Homework for Our Homes" exercises.

2. Discuss the chapter with another person.

If you are married, we urge you and your spouse to prioritize time each week to work on and discuss the exercises in this workbook.

However, if you are a single parent or your spouse is not available, we recommend you find a trusted friend, counselor, or pastor who is willing to be your **partner** as you work through this workbook.

Because it is not good for anyone to be alone (Genesis 2:18), we all need someone with whom we can share, cry, laugh, hurt, and be comforted. This is part of God's plan—no one alone.

A good partner is someone who *cares for us.* We're not going to share our hurt with someone unless we're convinced of that person's care for us. We need someone who will stay close enough to know what we're going through and someone who will consistently be available to help. We must sense that our partner cares for us just because of who we are, not because of what we do. It's good to know that in addition to God there is at least one other human who really cares for us.

This person should be someone *we can trust.* We'll be reluctant to vulnerably share our hurt with others unless we know we can trust them. A trustworthy partner must be committed to not talking about us to others without our permission, respond with compassion and acceptance to our hurts and pain, and not use anything we've shared against us.

Availability is also important. We may have friends who care about us and are trustworthy, but if they are not available when we need them, we'll still hurt alone. This is one of those times when availability is just as important as ability.

Do you have a caring, trustworthy, and available partner? As you begin this parenting journey, identify a special person who can share this experience with you. This might be your spouse, pastor, counselor, or a special friend within the body of Christ. If you're married, significant benefits will be experienced if both you and your spouse embark on the journey!

Take time now to think about who your partner is going to be. After giving prayerful consideration and talking with your partner candidate, write your partner's name here:

_____

The following "Personal Commitment" page clarifies what will be expected as you seek to make the most of your experience with this workbook. We suggest that you read it over carefully and discuss it with your partner before making this commitment.

Personal Commitment

1. I will set aside time each week to complete the individual exercises in this workbook, with honesty and sincerity.

2. I will prioritize time in my schedule for group meetings, discussing this material with my partner, and implementing principles with my child(ren).

3. I will participate in both the giving and receiving of support and care.

4. I will acknowledge and respect any differences in our stages of growth and will refrain from making comparisons with my partner or other families.

5. I will focus on my own thoughts, feelings, and actions rather than those of others as I seek to be accountable to God as the Divine Author of the family.

6. I will be open and willing for God to show me how I can relate more intimately with Him, and how I can meet needs in my partner's life and the life of each child.

Name: _____ Date:_____

Name: _____ Date:_____

Using the *Parenting With Intimacy* Workbook With a Class or Group

The majority of exercises in this workbook are designed to be done on your own or with your partner. However, you can gain a great deal by discussing what you're learning with others, especially with other parents.

A series of companion resources are designed to enhance your experience with this workbook in class or group settings:

Parenting with Intimacy Video Series

These video tapes feature David Ferguson, Terri Snead and Paul Warren teaching all eight chapters of Parenting with Intimacy. Each lesson is approximately 25 minutes in length. Small groups and classes often let the videos "teach" the group and then facilitators lead in group discussion. These videos also serve as supplemental resources for leader preparation.

Parenting with Intimacy Audio Series

Cassette tapes taken directly from the video series. Excellent for personal reinforcement of the content, "drive-time" preparation, exposing others to the principles, or as "make-up" for those who miss a class or group session.

Parenting with Intimacy Teaching Curriculum

Detailed lesson plans with specific learning objectives, reproducible masters, and supplemental ideas for each of eight chapters of the workbook. An invaluable tool for those who teach and lead classes and small groups.

Chapter 1

--- ■ ---

LET THE JOURNEY BEGIN!

(God's Design for Relationships)

Congratulations! You're about to embark on an exciting exploration of a new dimension of parenting—*parenting with intimacy.*

"Exploration? I didn't know I was signing on for an exploration. I was just looking for the latest *Top 10 Tips for Shaping Up Your Kids*!"

Don't panic. Take some deep breaths. You can do this. Admittedly, parenting with intimacy is not for the fainthearted, weak-kneed, or self-centered. It's hard work. But you're not afraid of hard work, are you?

> Truly knowing your child, allowing your child to know you, and becoming caringly involved in his or her life are the true keys for developing an intimate, loving relationship between parent and child.

"Well, no. I guess not."

Great! We're glad to have you on our journey. Rest assured, along the way we will be offering some of those "tips" you're seeking. And yet discipline, while an important aspect of parenting, is not the number-one issue.

Truly knowing your child, allowing your child to know you, and becoming caringly involved in his or her life are the true keys for developing an intimate, loving relationship between parent and child. Remember, loving your child is not a feeling—

it's an action. We're going to ask you to take action by digging deeper into relationships than you may have before.

What's that? No one told you to bring your excavation tools? Not to worry—we'll be sharing the important tools we all need for meaningful intimate relationships—relationships which reflect our love for God and for each other!

Before we get started, we'd like to introduce you to your traveling companions: The Warrens: Paul, Vicky and Matthew. The Fergusons: David, Teresa, Terri, Robin, and Eric. And the Sneads: Terri (Ferguson) Snead, her husband Wayne and their two sons, Brad and Michael. Throughout the ensuing pages, we'll be sharing true-life "Adventures in Parenting" of the Warrens, Fergusons, and Sneads—up close and personal.

It would be ego-enhancing to infer that we have "arrived" as parents. Ego-enhancing? Decidedly! Dishonest? Definitely! It's been said that confession is good for the soul but bad for the reputation. Be that as it may, we want you to know that we've made mistakes—lots of them! No one has parenting totally "figured out." We're all fellow-sojourners on this journey. Some may be a little farther along, but we're all still "works-in-progress."

Now that we've introduced ourselves, let the journey begin! First on our itinerary is an assessment of where we are—a "**priorities check**."

Priorities—everyone has them. Regardless of whether we've written ours down or even thought about them, we're living out what's important to us. When asked to list our priorities, most of us know some version of the "correct answer:" (1) God, (2) Family, (3) Ministry, (4) Work. We may pass this particular exam, but how are we doing on the "living exam?"

The following self-assessment tool will help us assess our true priorities. If we have to "hedge" our answers or if we respond with several "no's," we probably need to do some restructuring of our priorities. Let's ask ourselves, "What's going to genuinely matter ten years from now?" "What are the most important things in this life?"

Parenting with Intimacy
Self-Assessment Inventory

Yes	No		
___	___	1.	(If married) I spend meaningful, uninterrupted time alone with my spouse at least once a week.
___	___	2.	I spend uninterrupted "meaningful-to-my-children" time with each of my children at least once a week.
___	___	3.	I know who my children's friends are.
___	___	4.	I know what my children are doing in school.
___	___	5.	I know the stresses my children are experiencing.
___	___	6.	My spouse and children know me; I regularly share both joys and concerns with them.
___	___	7.	I am approachable to my spouse and family; they are not hesitant to vulnerably share their thoughts, opinions, and feelings with me or to approach me when I've offended them.
___	___	8.	I keep up with and give priority to family birthdays and other special family occasions.
___	___	9.	I spend regular, quality time deepening my intimate walk with God, seeking to experience the truth of His Word.
___	___	10.	I seek to model Christlikeness to others through my words and by my example, starting first with my own family.
___	___	11.	My checkbook, ministry commitments, TV, and reading habits reflect my love for God and devotion to my family.
___	___	12.	I often use my discretionary time to "enter into my family's world," doing what they want to do, seeking to mutually know and enjoy each other.

STOP AND CONSIDER

Review your responses to the twelve statements above and write out any changes in priorities that may be needed. *In order for me to truly know my spouse and children and develop intimacy with them, it will be important for me to give more time and attention to:*

_____

_____

_____

_____

_____

_____

_____

Take time to reflect on what you've just written. In a prayer, ask God for His guidance and strength. Write your thoughts and prayers to God here: (Ex: *Dear God, as I consider the changes I need to make, I need your guidance and strength to ...)*

_____

_____

_____

_____

_____

_____

_____

Now, let's get serious about these changes, knowing that, *"He who began a good work in you will perfect it until the day of Christ Jesus"* (Philippines 1:6). May the material in this workbook equip us to more fully live out God's priorities for our families!

God's Design
Born Needy!

A fundamental concept for parenting with intimacy is: **Every child and every parent has needs!**

We all come into this world needy, whether we want to admit it or not. God created each of us with physical, spiritual, and relational needs. In order to survive and thrive **physically**, we need at least air, food, water, shelter, and rest.

Spiritually, we all need eternal life, God's truth, fellowship with God and others, and because we sin, forgiveness. We don't survive and thrive spiritually apart from having these needs met!

> God directly meets our needs. And He also meets needs through other people.

Do we have any other kind of needs? Yes! God created us with other needs which can only be met relationally—needs which when met provide rich experiences of love and care. We call these *intimacy needs*.

As with physical and spiritual needs, because He loves us, God then provides for these needs to be met. How? He always directly meets our needs. And, He also meets these needs through other people.

For example, He tells us to give each other **acceptance**, just as He accepts us: "Accept one another, just as Christ has accepted you." By meeting our need for acceptance, He has validated that it's all right to need acceptance!

Another example, especially relevant when we are struggling with the inevitable pain of living in a fallen world with fallen people: According to II Corinthians 1:3-4, God ". . . comforts us in all our afflictions, so that we might comfort others with the comfort we ourselves have received from God." The fact that He comforts us means **comfort** is a legitimate human need.

Our needs for acceptance and comfort are not physical needs, nor are they spiritual needs. They are relational, *intimacy needs.*

Unfortunately, in our "pull-yourself-up-by-your-own-boot-straps," "you-better-take-care-of- yourself" culture, neediness conjures up visions of weakness and inappropriate dependency. Horror of horrors that we should be dependent on or need anyone!

But let's reason this out. If we're born needing something, are we selfish or weak because we need it? Think about it. Few people apologize for having physical needs—"I'm sorry to be using up so much air. I know it's selfish of me, but I just have this need to breathe." Sounds ridiculous, doesn't it? Yet many of us tend to feel guilty for having intimacy needs and conclude

---

The apostle Paul states confidently in Philippines 4:19, iAnd my God shall supply all your needs according to His riches in glory in Christ Jesus.i

---

that, if we do, we must be flawed in some way. This self-condemnation is based on a lie—that there must be something wrong with us if we have needs. If we believe this lie, we will end up either painfully self-condemned or we will try to pull off the "I don't need you" self-reliant, ruggedly individualistic lifestyle so exalted in our world.

The apostle Paul states confidently in Philippines 4:19, *"And my God shall supply all your needs according to His riches in glory in Christ Jesus."* How could he say this with such certainty if we're not supposed to have needs? The verse makes no sense apart from the reality that we all have needs that were placed within us by our Creator.

The truth is, we really need God, and He has created us to also need each other! It's OK to be needy, because God created us this way.

But has it always been that way? Or is our neediness the result of sin?

Let's travel all the way back to the Garden of Eden and take a look at the first human being..

Adam's Dilemma

In Genesis chapter one, on six different occasions God observed His creation and commented that what He saw "was good." But in Genesis chapter two, after creating Adam, God made a startling statement. For the first time in Scripture, He said, *"It is not good,"* (Genesis 2:18). And when God says something is not good, **it's not good!**

What's startling about this statement is that Adam seemed to have everything going for him:

◆ He had a *perfect environment*. No pollution, traffic jams, or diseases!
◆ He had an *exalted position*. God had given him dominion over His creation. He had no insecurities, jealousies, or pressure to perform. He was the C.E.O. of the Garden. According to modern-day standards, he was at the top of the ladder!
◆ He *possessed everything*. All of creation was there for his use and enjoyment! No problems with daily provision, monthly salaries, the IRS, or retirement plans. Everything that God had created was his (Genesis 1:28-30)!

So let's get this straight. Adam had a perfect environment, an exalted position, and unlimited resources, and yet God said, "It is not good." We live in a society that believes that these three areas are what you need to live a fulfilling life. So we strive for a more perfect job, a larger income, a bigger house, a higher position on the ladder of success in order to be happy. The lesson we can learn from Adam is that in spite of having all of these things, something was still missing. Something was not good.

Was there something wrong with his relationship with God? It may be a shock to realize that **even Adam's relationship with**

God was perfect—he had not yet sinned. He had intimacy with God!

So what in the world was "not good" about Adam's situation? What was his problem? Apparently just one thing: **Adam was alone. Adam needed a human relationship.**

A sovereign God, free to create Adam any way He desired, chose to fashion him in such a way that Adam needed to relate intimately to both God and other human beings. God had created Adam not only with physical and spiritual needs, but also with relational needs which Adam could not meet on his own. These needs could only be met through meaningful relationships with God and other people.

So what in the world was ìnot goodî about Adamís situation? What was his problem? Apparently just one thing: Adam was alone. Adam needed a human relationship.

In Genesis 2:18 God also declared that He would solve Adam's dilemma, and He did so by creating another human, someone with whom Adam could be intimate. God said, *"I will make a helper suitable for him."* God ministered to Adam's aloneness by giving him a human relationship, Eve.

There are two very important concepts to embrace here:
◆ God created Adam, so his aloneness and subsequent need for relationships were no accident or flaw in design. Nor were they the result of sin—since sin doesn't even enter the picture until later as recorded in Genesis 3.
◆ God provided for Adam's aloneness (he met his need) through Eve.

Thus we can reasonably draw the following conclusions:
◆ It must be OK to have needs.
◆ It must be OK (and, in fact, important to God) to have our needs met.

- God is committed to meet our needs—both directly and through others.
- God established marriage as one of the relationships through which He ministers to our needs. Later, he established families (Genesis 4, Psalm 127) and then close friendships ("fellowship") among His people within His church (Matthew 16).
- God can be trusted to meet our needs—and our needs will challenge us to exercise faith.
- God wants to involve us in giving to the needs of others— out of our gratefulness for the abundance of His provision for us.

These conclusions provide insight into establishing and maintaining intimate relationships. Intimate relationships involve deeply "knowing" another person, just as God deeply knew the inner aloneness of Adam. And they require caring involvement at the point of need, just as God ministered to Adam's need. So, as we begin our journey in parenting with intimacy, we will be challenged to truly *know* our children and to become *caringly involved* in giving to their intimacy needs (acceptance, comfort, and several others).

STOP AND CONSIDER

Take a moment and write down any thoughts or reactions you may have to the concept of your "neediness." We've proposed that all of us are created with certain physical, relational, and spiritual needs. We have suggested that we all need both God and other people. How do these key concepts strike you? What response(s) come to mind?

Be sure to share your reflections with your spouse or partner!

Unwrap Your Gift!

Imagine being presented with an exquisitely-wrapped package. You receive it with thanks and proceed to carefully place it on the shelf. Six months later the giver returns to your home and is disheartened upon observing that the gift has remained unopened. What would be the logical conclusion? You're uninterested and unappreciative. You've taken the gift—and the giver—for granted and missed a tremendous blessing. What a waste!

Psalm 127:3 says, *"Behold, children are a gift from the Lord."*

An integral part of parenting with intimacy is taking your child—your gift—untying the bow, undoing the wrapping, enjoying and getting to know this child deeply and intimately.

Don't miss this: A crucial step in the process of ¡unwrapping our gift¡ is understanding your child¡s intimacy needs and how these needs can be met.

This workbook is designed to help us as parents do just that. Unwrap your gift carefully—with a sense of awe—that you have been entrusted with such a treasure!

Remember bringing your newborn home from the hospital? It wasn't long before you realized that the little bundle of joy needed more than just air, food, and water. Baby's cry often signaled a different type of need: "Mommy/Daddy, I need to be held, rocked, cuddled. I need attention. I need to be comforted." Our intimacy needs cry out for someone to be attentive, to take the initiative to become caringly involved.

The rest of this chapter will identify and define ten key intimacy needs and offer some practical ways that we can meet these needs in the lives of our children. We'll also see how meeting needs was an important part of Jesus' ministry and how God continually meets these needs in our lives.

Ten Key Intimacy Needs

Acceptance: Receiving another person willingly and unconditionally, especially when the other's behavior has been imperfect. Being willing to continue loving another in spite of offenses. (Romans 15:7)

Affection: Expressing care and closeness through (non-sexual) physical touch; saying "I love you." (Romans 16:16; Mark 10:16)

Appreciation: Expressing thanks, praise or commendation. Recognizing accomplishment or effort. (Colossians 3:15b; I Corinthians 11:2)

Approval (Blessing): Building up or affirming another; affirming both the fact of and the importance of a relationship. (Ephesians 4:29; Mark 1:11)

Attention: Conveying appropriate interest, concern, and care; taking thought of another; entering another's "world." (I Corinthians 12:25)

Comfort: Responding to a hurting person with words, feelings, and touch; to hurt with and for another's grief or pain. (Romans 12:15b; Matthew 5:4; II Corinthians 1:3-4; John 11:35)

Encouragement: Urging another to persist and persevere toward a goal; stimulating toward love and good deeds. (I Thessalonians 5:11; Hebrews 10:24)

Respect: Valuing and regarding another highly; treating another as important; honoring another. (Romans 12:10)

Security (Peace): Harmony in relationships; freedom from fear or threat of harm. (Romans 12:16,18)

Support: Coming alongside and gently helping with a problem or struggle; providing appropriate assistance. (Galatians 6:2)

Now let's consider each of these needs in more depth, and especially how we might give to meet these needs in our children's lives:

Acceptance

Receiving another person willingly and unconditionally, especially when the other's behavior has been imperfect. Being willing to continue loving another in spite of offenses (Romans 15:7).

The human heart cries out for acceptance. "Don't insist that everything about me be like you or anyone else. Accept me as significant, unique; love me for who I am, in spite of my behavior. Don't equate my *worth* to you with my *performance*. Demonstrate your love toward me *while I'm yet a sinner*!"

Here are some practical ways to demonstrate acceptance. Quickly forgive your children when they offend you. A lack of forgiveness short-circuits acceptance. Don't pout, reject, or ignore them as punishment. Our need for acceptance is accentuated when we experience a failure or disappointment. Notice when your children experience disappointments or failures (real or perceived) and minister to their need for acceptance. Give empathy—don't minimize, ignore, or ridicule your child's pain. Acceptance is based upon a person's innate value to God as a person of special worth and not on their performance or productivity.

Love your children with God's unmerited, unconditional, and unlimited love. God's love for us is unmerited (we don't deserve it and can't earn it), unconditional (it's not based on what we do or don't do), and unlimited (it will never "run out" or be detained). We should accept and love others in like manner.

Jesus met our ultimate need for acceptance in that *"while we were yet sinners"* He died for us (Rom. 5:8). He looked beyond our faults and saw and met our needs. During His earthly ministry, Jesus accepted people where they were regardless of background, race, or condition; helped them deal with their failures; loved people with unconditional love; and forgave freely.

STOP AND CONSIDER

How is your child different from you? (Consider each child individually.) What are the areas that are the most difficult for you to accept about your child?

_____
_____
_____
_____
_____
_____

How have you shown acceptance to your child lately? Have you communicated that you love your child even if he doesn't change? Have you shown love that isn't connected with performance? Write recent demonstrations of acceptance here:

_____
_____
_____
_____
_____
_____
_____

Affection

Expressing care and closeness through (non-sexual) physical touch; saying "I love you" (Romans 16:16; Mark 10:16).

Affection can be expressed by looking into your child's eyes and verbalizing your love: "I really love you!"

It's also giving hugs and kisses. Little children run around with their arms out wanting to be hugged—"Hold me! Cuddle me! Rock me! Touch me!"

As kids grow older, it often becomes "uncool" to admit one's need for these things, but the need is there nonetheless. Parents can be tempted to reduce their affection as kids appear not to "enjoy" it. Resist this temptation! Continue to show affection through touch and hugs—even if they're going through a stage where they don't hug back. Continue to offer affection in age-appropriate ways and doses. Verbalize your love at times of celebration and disappointment. Notes of loving care are great for teenagers. Send e-mail from the office or drop a card in the mail. It's never "uncool" to enjoy getting mail!

During His earthly ministry, Jesus felt free to touch others affectionately. He sometimes healed people, touching them in the process (Matthew 8:3, 8:15, 9:29). He reassured His frightened disciples accompanied by physical expression (Matthew 17:7). He ministered to children through physical affection (Mark 10:16, Matthew 19:13). Through out the pages of Scripture, God verbalizes His love and care for His people (Isaiah 40:11, John 3:16, Ephesians 5:1-2, I Peter 5:7 and many others).

STOP AND CONSIDER

Which of your children could benefit from more affection? Who gives the most hugs and "I love you's" in the family? Who wants to receive hugs and "I loves you's?"

_____
_____
_____
_____
_____
_____

How have you shown love recently through gentle touch and tender words? Have you hugged your son recently? Have you told your daughter that you love her? Write about some recent occasions:

_____

_____

_____

_____

_____

_____

Appreciation

Expressing thanks, praise or commendation. Recognizing accomplishment or effort (Colossians 3:15b; I Corinthians 11:2).

Meeting children's need for appreciation requires thought and effort. Because of the seemingly endless demands on our time and energy, we may tend to focus on correcting our kids only, rather than looking for ways to express appreciation. Misbehavior does need to be addressed and dealt with appropriately, but kids also need to hear an occasional "Well done!" and "Thank you" when appropriate choices are made. No parent wants to feel taken for granted—Kids are no different!

Appreciation might sound like this: "I really appreciate the way you took care of your younger brother this afternoon. I know you had other things you could have done with your friends that would have been more fun. You're a great big brother and a wonderful son."

"I've noticed how much effort you've been putting into keeping your room picked up this week. I really appreciate your helpfulness. It feels great that we're all a team."

God met our ultimate need for appreciation as the Bible affirms us as saints and joint-heirs (Romans 1:7, 8:17) and royal priests and people for God's own possession in I Peter (I Peter 2:9). During His earthly ministry, Jesus continually voiced appreciation to individuals: the Canaanite woman (Matthew 15:28), Mary of Bethany (Mark 14:6), a Roman Centurion (Luke 7:9), and He commended John the Baptist to others (Luke 7:28). Finally, God has promised ultimately to appreciate and reward all who are faithful (Matthew 26:34-40, I Corinthians 4:1-5, 2 Timothy 4:8 and many others).

STOP AND CONSIDER

Make a list of things that each of your children have recently done, for which you could express appreciation.

_____

_____

_____

_____

_____

How have you communicated appreciation lately? When was the last time you thanked your son? praised your daughter? When have you noticed their efforts and said, "Great job!"?

_____

_____

_____

_____

Approval (Blessing)

Building up or affirming another; affirming both the fact of and the importance of a relationship (Ephesians 4:29; Mark 1:11).

Affirm your children privately and publicly as being of great value to you and to God. Acknowledge them privately and in public for *who they are*—not just for *what they do.* This is the difference between a human "being" and a human "doing."

"I'm sure proud that you're my daughter."

"You're my beloved son in whom I am well pleased!"

"God could not have given me a more special son/daughter."

Identify character strengths of each child and praise them for these qualities: "Bill, you are one of the most responsible people I know! Your diligence and thoroughness are excellent qualities." (See list of qualities on page 133 for possible qualities to commend your children for.) Our approval for character qualities helps free them from having to seek approval by competing with siblings or other peers. As children grow in the security of parents' approval, they experience freedom to grow and mature without fear of failure.

God the Father met His Son Jesus' need for expressed approval at His baptism: "You are my Son, whom I love; with you I am well pleased!" (Mark 1:11). He affirmed the **fact** of their relationship ("You are my Son") and the **importance** of their relationship (You are my beloved Son). And God has met our ultimate need for approval, affirming us as saints (Rom. 1:7), sons of the Most High (Eph. 1:5), joint-heirs with Christ (Rom. 8:17), royal priests, and people for God's own possession (I Peter 2:9), and as His dearly loved children (Ephesians 5:1, I John 3:1).

Stop and Consider

What is special about each of your children? What are the character traits of your son or daughter that make you proud?

_____

_____

_____

_____

_____

How have you met your child's need for approval recently?
Have you told her you are proud of her? Have you told him how
blessed you are to have such a special son? How have you
expressed the pleasure of having/receiving your child?

_____

_____

_____

_____

_____

_____

Attention

**Conveying appropriate interest, concern, and care; taking
thought of another; entering another's "world"
(I Corinthians 12:25).**

Whatever their age, it's impossible to meet our children's
need for attention without entering their world and investing
the valuable commodity of T-I-M-E.

Several years ago, Josh McDowell Ministries conducted a
monumental study in which they surveyed 3,795 church-
attending youths (**Right from Wrong**, McDowell & Hostetler,
1994). Each youth completed a confidential survey on a variety
of topics.

The results were startling! These youth reported spending
under four minutes a day in meaningful conversation with their
mothers and two-and-a-half minutes a day talking things over
with dad. Sadly, far more time was likely spent disciplining
these youth than was reportedly invested in meaningful time
getting to know them!

Our world is raising a generation of children whose concept
of "father" is a person they do not know and who does not know
them, entering their world to "discipline" them. Ephesians 6:4
admonishes fathers not to provoke their children to wrath. One
of the quickest ways to provoke children to wrath is to discipline them without first establishing a loving relationship with

them. In fact, enforcing rules without the foundation of an intimate relationship frequently leads to a child's rebellion.

It's impossible to truly know our children without spending time with them—entering into *their* world. Jesus gave us the perfect example when He chose to give up His position in heaven and entered into our world so that He could know us and we could know Him. As parents, we are similarly challenged to leave our adult world of work, career, hobbies, ministry, and friends to enter into a child's world:

◆ a world of make-believe, stories, and toys
◆ a world of play, silly games, and laughter
◆ a world of technology, thrill-seeking, and heartaches
◆ a world of disappointment, "strange music," and insecurities

---

STOP AND CONSIDER

What is your child's "world?" Is she into nail polish, dolls, or soccer? Does he like video games, baseball, or dinosaurs? For each child, name at least three aspects of that child's world:

_____

_____

_____

_____

_____

How have you met the need for attention lately? How have you entered his/her world or done what he/she likes to do? Write about some recent occasions:

_____

_____

_____

_____

How might you more consistently invest time with each of your children, entering their worlds in ways they would enjoy and find meaningful?

_____
_____
_____
_____
_____
_____

Comfort

Responding to a hurting person with words, feelings, and touch; to hurt with and for another's grief or pain. (Romans 12:15b; Matthew 5:4; II Corinthians 1:3-4; John 11:35)

Sit on a bench at any playground and you'll observe a perfect example of a child's need for comfort. When children fall down, they typically look around to see if anyone's watching. If they find an empathetic witness to their plight, do they say, "No big deal!" and go right back to playing? Hardly! They pucker up and open the floodgates! If the observer happens to be a loved one, the child will usually rush into their arms for a hug, some cuddling, and a kiss to "make it all better." Hurting children not only need the physical expression of comfort, they need to hear comforting words as well. The message might sound like, "I'm sorry you're hurting. I'm here for you."

But what does comforting really look like? Here's a short interaction between mother and daughter which illustrates what this need is and how it can be met:

When Lucy's mom picked her up from school, Lucy's dress was torn, her knees skinned, and her cheeks streaked with tears.

"Lucy, sweetheart, what happened?" her mother asked. (So far, so good.)

Haltingly, between sobs, Lucy replied, "Sarah pushed me down on the playground and called me a name in front of all my friends."

What does Lucy most need to experience with her mother at that moment? Comforting words like, "Honey, I know how much that must have hurt your feelings. I'm sorry that happened, and I feel sad that you're hurting." She needs for her mother to take her into her arms and hold her, lovingly soothing her body and spirit.

What does Lucy NOT need from her mother? "Well, what did you do to make her to do that? I'm sure you must have done something to provoke her!" She also does not need: "That little brat! I'm going to call her mother about this!" or "Well now honey, don't cry. This is no big deal. You're not that hurt!" or "I'm sure Sarah was just having a bad day. Somebody was probably mean to her, too." These kinds of responses inflict even more pain through minimizing, blame, and condemnation.

What an irony—when loved ones are hurting they don't need what we often are most inclined to give: facts, logic, advice, criticism. What they need is *comfort*—an emotional expression that we care—weeping with those who weep, mourning with and for those who mourn.

Jesus ministered comfort throughout His earthly ministry, often identifying with the hurts of others to the degree that He wept with and for them (John 11:35, Luke 19:41). Even on the eve of His death, Jesus comforted His disciples (John 14:1,18; 16:33).

We are reminded that God is the "Father of compassion and the God of all comfort" (II Corinthians 1:3) and the Holy Spirit is often referred to as the "Comforter" as in the Gospel of John 14:16, and John 15:26.

Stop and Consider

When your child is hurting are you tempted to respond with logic, advice, or even criticism, instead of simply giving comfort? Explain your thoughts here:

_____

_____

_____

_____

_____

How have you given comfort to your child recently? When have you eased hurts with your tender words and listening ear? When have you let them know you care about the things that cause them pain? When have you said, "I'm sorry that happened. I feel sad when you are sad."

_____

_____

_____

_____

_____

Encouragement

Urging to persist and persevere toward a goal; stimulating toward love and good deeds (I Thessalonians 5:11; Hebrews 10:24).

All children need a fan club; and the most active members of their club need to be their mom and dad. When parents are cheering them on, it provides a tremendous impetus that propels them toward reaching a goal. Give them your wholehearted blessing to reach for the stars.

Kids need the obvious heart-to-heart conversations in which we spur them on in the face of discouragement, but just as important are the more covert messages of encouragement: the "You can do it!" notes mom leaves on the refrigerator door, or the "Son, I have confidence in you!" note that dad leaves on the dashboard of the car. Encouragement might be a special night out, a timely phone call, or a loving prayer prayed on another's behalf.

God meets our need for encouragement by providing us with an abundant life through Christ (John 10:10) and by promising us that He will never leave us or forsake us (Hebrews 13:5). During His earthly ministry, Jesus continually encouraged His disciples and those who were downcast and discouraged. He appeared to the men on the Emmaus road and to the disciples gathered in Jerusalem—and in so doing, removed their feelings of hopelessness and discouragement (Luke 24:13-53). God continually encourages us through the ministry of His word, the presence of His Spirit, and answered prayer.

STOP AND CONSIDER

What goals or wishes have your children identified? What areas of discouragement or disappointment have your children encountered?

(For instance, Elizabeth has talked about wanting to try out for the basketball team; Jeremy was really discouraged last week when he discovered the price for the stereo system. His savings plan just got extended; Erin showed interest in swimming lessons this year.)

_____

_____

_____

How have you urged your child to persist and persevere? Write about a recent time you have built her/him up and inspired her/him toward a goal. Write about a recent time when you've said words like, "You can do it. You can do anything God wants you to do through Christ who strengthens you!"

_____

_____

_____

_____

Respect

Valuing and regarding another highly; treating another as important; honoring another (Romans 12:10).

The need for respect is not something that magically appears when a person turns twenty-one. We all need to be valued—God says we are to honor one another! From day one, even small children need respect.

Every child is a unique creation of God. Their value is greater than just being the son or daughter of their earthly parents. They're on loan from God, and He has a special plan for each of them. Part of meeting your child's need for respect is recognizing that many of their characteristics are part of their unique design. (Chapter 3 will address this in more detail.)

Children also need to experience respect in at least three distinct areas: their feelings, their opinions, and their possessions. They need to hear from their parents:

> *"I'm listening. Your thoughts and feelings are very important to me."*
>
> *"We'd like to know what you'd like to do on Saturday. We value your input."*
>
> *"I understand your need for privacy and your need to have things that belong to you."*
>
> *"Shawn, you need to ask your brother's permission before you play with his toys."*

During His earthly ministry, Jesus ignored all the social prejudices of His society by showing respect to tax collectors, Samaritans, the poor, lepers, and women. He treated all people as those with intrinsic value and worth—created in God's image. And let's not forget that He valued us so much that He was even willing to die for us!

STOP AND CONSIDER

What would respect "look like" to each of your children? What feelings and opinions have they expressed recently? Have these been heard, received, considered? Have there been disagreements or conflicts about personal property? Could these conflicts stem from a lack of respect?

_____

_____

_____

_____

_____

_____

How have you recently shown respect to your children? What have you done to affirm their intrinsic worth? How have you shown respect for her/his feelings? opinions? possessions? When have you said something like, "I'd like to hear your ideas" or "I want to understand your feelings and perspectives"?

_____

_____

_____

_____

_____

_____

Security (Peace)

Harmony in relationships; freedom from fear or threat of harm (Romans 12:16, 18).

The world is a scary place to live, especially if you're a kid. Violence, destruction, and danger are all around us and are constantly portrayed in the media. All kids, are aware of families that are being torn apart by divorce, violence, drugs and/or abuse; and that brings added worries and fears. Your child needs to know that even though your family goes through tough times, you are committed to one another and to solving problems together.

It might be as simple as a Dad verbalizing at the dinner table, "Kids, I was just thinking today about how special your mom is. I'm sure glad she's my wife!" (As Dad kisses Mom, the kids are blessed by the security of their parents' commitment to each other and to them.) This declaration of love "casts out fear" (1 John 4:18-19.

A single parent could declare, "I know we've been through some challenging times, but I want you to know that I'm more committed than ever to love, protect, and care for you."

Financial and physical issues can also relate to security needs. Parents provide financial security for their children by operating on a budget, adhering to scriptural principles of finances, providing an adequate income, and planning for future financial responsibilities. Physical security needs are met when parents make sure the doors are locked at night, seat belts are fastened, and rules are enforced to prevent physical harm.

Although they may deny it, kids derive a sense of security from knowing where the limits are and knowing there are people in their lives who care enough to set rules and actually enforce the limits through loving discipline. Therefore, appropriately disciplining our children ministers to their need for security. We shouldn't hold our breath waiting for them to thank us, but we can be confident that we are, indeed, meeting one of their deepest needs.

During His earthly ministry, Jesus offered security to those who were close to Him by continually meeting their physical, relational, and spiritual needs. At times He even performed a miracle to meet physical needs such as the need for food (feeding of the five thousand.) God meets our need for security by promising never to leave us or forsake us (Joshua 1:5, Matthew 28:20). He has committed to meet needs for food, clothing, and shelter (Matthew 6:25-32), and those who trust Christ as Savior have the security of spending eternity with Him (John 10:28).

STOP AND CONSIDER

Which of your children have felt insecure about finances, physical safety, changes in plans, or the harmony of relationships? Who may be feeling exposed to physical or emotional danger?

_____

_____

_____

_____

_____

How have you recently reassured your children about the harmony in your relationships? How do you demonstrate your commitment not to harm your child physically or emotionally? How often do you take initiative to meet your daughter's/son's need for security? When have you said words like, "I'm here for you." or "I promise to take care of you?" How have you recently helped them work through one of their fears or insecurities? Write your thoughts here:

_____

_____

_____

_____

_____

Support

Coming alongside and gently helping with a problem or struggle; providing appropriate assistance (Galatians 6:2).

Kids need a partner who will walk alongside them to help navigate the hazards on their path toward maturity. This does not mean completely shouldering the load for them. In the long run, doing so would actually become a hindrance rather than help because it would convey the message, "This is too scary, too difficult for you. You'd better stand aside while I take over." But neither should it mean standing at a distance while your child struggles alone. Rather, offering support involves conveying, both through words and actions, that you are with your child—that you want to assist with the heavy loads—no matter what. Looking down the road towards maturity can be a frightening prospect. Your child needs to know he won't be traveling alone.

God met our ultimate need for support by anticipating the great burden that we could not bear ourselves (the payment for our sins), and by providing for us through the life and death of His Son, Jesus Christ. During His earthly ministry, Jesus invited the multitudes to "*Come to Me, all you who are weary and burdened, and I will give you rest.*" (Matthew 11:28). When Jesus completed His earthly ministry, the Holy Spirit was given to believers as the "One called alongside" who supports us, comforts us, guides us and intercedes for us (John 16:12-15, Acts 9:31, John 14:16, Romans 8:14, and Romans 8:26).

STOP AND CONSIDER

What challenges and struggles are your children experiencing? (For instance, Jill is trying to decide which college to attend; Joey is struggling with his Science Fair project; Amanda wants to learn to play tennis.)

_____

_____

_____

_____

_____

_____

How might you come alongside your child to assist with a current problem or struggle?

_____

_____

_____

_____

_____

_____

_____

The Priority of Needs Is Different for Every Individual

While we all seem to have the same needs, the *priority* of those needs is different for each person. Your greatest need may be for *affection*, while your partner's greatest need may be *security*. One child may have an acute need for *comfort* while her sibling's greatest need may be *approval*.

If we're not careful, we'll treat everyone as if they have the same priority of needs. We might also try to meet other's needs based on our own priority. For instance, if your greatest need is for affection, you may gallantly and sincerely inundate your partner with affection without realizing that it may be at the bottom of his/her own needs list. You might become somewhat indignant if your partner isn't overwhelmed with gratefulness for your affectionate giving. It would be an innocent, well-meaning mistake, but a mistake nonetheless.

An important aspect of learning to love individuals as individuals, particularly our spouse and children, is taking time to know them and to discover their unique priority of needs. This is perhaps part of what Peter meant when he admonished husbands to, "*Live with your wives in an understanding way*" (1 Peter 3:7). It may also be a part of how a woman, "*Looks well to the ways of her household*" (Proverbs 31:27). It seems like an important part of truly getting to know our children as we unwrap them as "gifts from the Lord" (Psalm 127:3). God's plan for our lives involves a connectedness with one another. We need to relate to each other in a close and loving way. Intimacy is spawned, maintained, and deepened when we, in humility and faith, draw upon God's unlimited resources and then lovingly give to meet one another's needs.

Applying the Principles

Review the descriptions of the Top Ten Intimacy Needs. Then, keeping in mind the uniqueness of each child, fill in your "guess" as to each child's top three needs. Have your partner fill in his/her "guess" as well.

You might also spend time reviewing your own top three needs and the needs of your spouse (if married). After discovering each person's priority of needs, as a family, look for ways to meet other's needs.

Acceptance	Comfort
Affection	Encouragement
Appreciation	Respect
Approval	Security
Attention	Support

Child's Name   **My Guess of Top 3 Needs**

Ex: Andrew   attention   comfort   approval

_____   _____   _____   _____

_____   _____   _____   _____

_____   _____   _____   _____

Child's Name   **Partner's Guess of Top 3 Needs**

_____   _____   _____   _____

_____   _____   _____   _____

_____   _____   _____   _____

_____   _____   _____   _____

Child's Name   **Child's Indication of Top 3 Needs**

_____   _____   _____   _____

_____   _____   _____   _____

_____   _____   _____   _____

_____   _____   _____   _____

[For further evaluation of your family's intimacy needs refer to **The Intimacy Needs Assessment Tool** in the Appendix.]

If Any Of You Lacks Wisdom

Parenting with intimacy is an awesome calling. As you begin your journey, ask the Lord for wisdom. He promises in James 1:5 to give it generously and without reproach. He knows we need Him and is just waiting for us to invite Him to be our constant companion and omniscient guide. He's the only One who knows what lies ahead. He knows every bend and curve in the road, every pothole, every detour. Don't start your journey without Him.

> *"If any of you lacks wisdom, he should ask God, who gives generously to all without finding fault, and it will be given to him."James 1:5*

Special Thoughts for Single Parents

As a single parent, be sure to replenish your own emotional "bank account." We understand the enormous pain of trying to remove a child's aloneness while experiencing loneliness yourself. Involving yourself in positive adult activities, support networks, and Christ-centered friendships will help remove your aloneness. Maintaining these relationships will allow God and others to minister to you and your needs. Keeping your emotional resources at an optimum level will enable you to continue giving lovingly to your children.

Special Thoughts for Blended Families

There's a normal but mistaken tendency to try to compensate for a broken home by prioritizing the children. Prioritize your marriage relationship, then give to your children. Children from divorced homes have already experienced the loss of security that results when an adult man and woman cease to sacrificially and permanently love one another. As a blended family you now have the opportunity to minister to this loss by reaffirming the secure relationships between married partners.

Therefore, make it a priority to meet your spouse's intimacy needs.

Children of a blended family often experience the pain of aloneness when there's a loss of a parent or sibling due to divorce or death. This aloneness isn't removed just because there are more people in the house. Make a conscious effort to talk to your children about missing a loved one. Let them know it's OK to be sad and share words of comfort for their loss.

Experiencing Biblical Truth

"But that the members (of the body) should have the same care for one another."
I Corinthians 12:25

1. Complete the following sentence: *I feel loved, cared for, and special when . . .*

   _____

   _____

   _____

   _____

   _____

   _____

   _____

   For example: *I feel loved, cared for, and special when someone helps me with the chores around the house.* (Or) *I feel loved, cared for, and special when my wife gives me a kiss for no particular reason.*

2. Review the list of Ten Key Intimacy Needs again, noting the definitions.

3. What relationship do you see between your response to question #1 and the three or four needs you have checked? Share your reflections with your spouse or partner:

   _____

   _____

   _____

   _____

   _____

   _____

   _____

   _____

   For example: *I feel loved when someone helps me with the chores because my need for support is being met—That's one of the needs I checked as important. (Or,) I feel loved when my wife gives me a kiss because of my need for affection. Affection is one of my priority needs.*

Homework For Our Homes

1. Ask each of your children to finish the sentence: *"I feel Mommy's/Daddy's love when..."* Older children might finish the sentence: *"I feel loved and cared for when..."*
2. Consider each child's answer—To what extent do their responses correspond to your guess of their three or four priority needs?
3. Look for opportunities to show love to each child this week. Make sure your demonstration of love matches the way they finished the sentence above.

But what if my children are very young? How do I know which needs are most important and how to meet them?

Key Intimacy Needs for Infants, Toddlers, and Pre-schoolers and How to Meet Them

It may be difficult to identify the most important needs of children under the age of five since they are still in the midst of rapid change and development! It may also seem as if your child needs all ten all of the time! Listed below are the ten intimacy needs and what it might "look like" to meet those needs. Take heart! You may already be meeting these needs significantly on a daily basis!

Acceptance: Receiving another person willingly and unconditionally, especially when the other's behavior has been imperfect. Being willing to continue a relationship in spite of offenses (Romans 15:7).

Looks like: letting your infant touch your nose, mouth, and eyes while feeding; giving your toddler opportunities to explore; receiving his curiosity as a gift from God; showing tolerance of your preschooler's messes; greeting your child each morning with a smile and cheerful, pleasant words.

Affection: Expressing care and closeness through physical touch; saying "I love you" (Romans 16:16).

Looks like: cuddling; stroking your child's cheek, smiling; kissing fingers, toes and tummy; playing "I'm gonna get you" as you nuzzle your baby's tummy with your head; playing "This little piggy"; saying "I love you." Wrestling on the floor.

Appreciation: Expressing thanks, praise or commendation. Recognizing accomplishment or effort (Colossians 3:15b; I Corinthians 11:2).

Looks like: saying thank you for sharing a bit of cookie; sharing a toy or taking turns; giving a sticker for a job well done or for good effort; noticing when your child obeys a rule, uses the potty, or brings you trash to throw away and then praising and thanking the child.

Approval: Building up or affirming others for who they are; affirming both the fact of and the importance of a relationship (Ephesians 4:29; Mark 1:11).

Looks like: using a warm, loving tone of voice; using positive, affirming words when you describe your child to others; singing to your child and singing with your child. "You're Mommy's precious baby." "You're Daddy's big boy!" "Your are a special present from God to Mommy and Daddy!"

Attention: Conveying appropriate interest, concern, and care; taking thought of another; entering another's "world" (I Corinthians 12:25).

Looks like: distinguishing between a hungry cry, a tired cry, and a distress cry and responding appropriately to meet the need; cooing and babbling with your baby; playing "peek-a-boo"; playing with blocks or bubbles or whatever your child likes to play; occasionally initiating play with your child, rather than always waiting for him to ask. Listening carefully to what your child is saying, without interrupting or finishing sentences; giving undivided focus.

Comfort: Coming alongside with word, feeling, and touch; to hurt with and for another's grief or pain (Romans 12:15b).

Looks like: snuggling or holding close when your child is upset; holding your baby securely; using a soft, soothing tone of voice; giving your child a massage; rocking your baby; singing a lullaby; rubbing your toddler's back so she can go to sleep; kissing a hurt. Saying, "I feel sad for you that you were hurt!" Crying with your child.

Encouragement: Urging toward persistence and perseverance; stimulating toward love and good deeds (I Thessalonians 5:11; Hebrews 10:24).

Looks like: cheering for your child as your he or she tries something new; opening your arms and urging your toddler to take his first steps toward you; saying words like, "I know you can do it! Give it a try! You'll do fine! Let me see you do it!"

Respect: Valuing and regarding another highly; treating another as important; honoring others (Romans 12:10).

Looks like: apologizing to your preschooler when you "blow it."; eliminating sarcasm and hostility from your voice; using a positive tone of voice with a pleasant attitude. Keeping your promises. Responding promptly when your child needs you.

Security: Harmony in relationships; freedom from fear or threat of harm (Romans 12:16,18).

Looks like: setting appropriate limits for a child's age and then being consistent with them; holding your infant and being confident but relaxed in the way you hold her; establishing routines for sleeping, eating, and playing. Providing a safe, "child-proof" environment in your home. Making rules, requirements, and expectations clear in advance, especially for new situations. Being careful who your child is with.

Support: Coming alongside and gently helping with a problem or struggle; providing appropriate assistance (Galatians 6:2).

Looks like: mimicking your baby's sounds and taking turns in conversation, thus assisting with language development; teaching your toddler how to walk, march, or jump; doing hard things together like putting on shoes, getting dressed, learning colors and shapes.

Chapter 2

———— ∎ ————

UNDERSTANDING
INTIMACY NEEDS
(THE FOUNDATION FOR PARENTING WITH INTIMACY)

The Case of the Soccer Ball-Eating Tree

One steamy Sunday afternoon, six-year-old Eric burst through the back door. "Dad! Dad! Remember that cartoon where there was a kite-eating tree?"

David looked up from the outline he was preparing for his parenting class at church that evening.

"Yes, Eric, I remember."

"Well, Dad. We have a soccer ball-eating tree in our backyard! It ate my ball and won't give it back! You need to come outside and get it out!"

For a fleeting moment David entertained the thought, "Not now, Eric. Can't you see I'm busy preparing for my parenting class?" Laughing to himself at the irony, David took Eric's hand and they headed off to confront the Goliath-like cottonwood tree that had devoured Eric's ball.

The tree was humongous!! Their only hope was to throw something into the tree to knock the ball loose. For the next hour they used every available means to get that stubborn, stingy old tree to cough up the ball. At one point, the tree was the proud owner of not just the soccer ball but a tennis ball, a tennis racket, a baseball, a baseball bat, and a garden hose. As David pitched each item at the entrenched soccer ball, Eric coached gleefully from the sidelines, "No, Dad. Too far to the left! A little more to the right! Almost, Dad! Too high! Too low! Try again!"

Finally, persistence paid off. Eric's ball was rescued. Father and son stood victorious—drenched with perspiration, but victorious nonetheless.

In this chapter, we're embarking on an exploration of the **needs principle**—the impact needs have on our lives.

Remember, God could have created us any way He desired. Thus, He could have made us not needing each other! He could have designed us to be just fine without receiving attention, affection, appreciation, comfort, support or other intimacy needs from anyone. Yet He chose to make us physically, spiritually, and relationally needy. What is the relevance of our neediness and that of our children?

It works like this:

- Needs met = satisfaction, contentment, being loved and cared for— **Experienced Intimacy**
- Needs unmet = frustration, anxiety, dissatisfaction, not being cared for— **Experienced Pain**

To illustrate the validity of the Needs Principle, consider some of our physical needs. We have a need for sleep, and after a good night's sleep we feel refreshed, satisfied and contented. However, several days of sleep deprivation will leave us feeling edgy, irritable, and frustrated. The same applies to our need for food. Following a good meal you feel gratified and fulfilled; but if you go for an extended period of time without eating, you're likely to feel weak, discontented, touchy, and frustrated.

If this principle applies to physical needs, doesn't it stand to reason it would also apply to intimacy needs? The answer to that is a resounding yes! If our needs for attention, approval, appreciation, etc. are neglected, we'll likely experience pain. But when these needs are met, we experience blessing. Our God-given needs are so strong and persistent that they will influence how we think, feel, and eventually behave.

STOP AND CONSIDER

Imagine that you have just shared a difficult life struggle with your best friend. You're feeling especially down this day and were really counting on your friend to listen, to express care. But instead of a caring response, your friend cuts you short, saying, "Look, everyone has hard times—I've got to go."

What might you be **thinking** at that moment? (Ex: "I really needed to talk with him. I can't believe he said that! I wonder what I did wrong?") _____

_____

_____

What might you be **feeling**? (Ex: hurt, offended, angry)

_____

What might you "**do**" in response? How might your **behavior** be affected? (Ex: "I'd keep myself busy so I don't have to think about it." Or, "I'd probably call up another friend and talk about what a jerk the other person was," etc.)_____

_____

_____

What **needs** may have gone unmet for you in this situation? (comfort? support? others? See Key Intimacy Needs list from Chapter 1)

_____

_____

Yes, when our needs are neglected or abused, a downward spiral can be set into motion:

Needs Unmet ▶ Faulty Thinking ▶ Painful Emotions ▶
Unproductive Behavior

Stop and Consider

Let's replay the previous scenario, but this time your friend responds differently. What if you shared a difficult life struggle with your best friend and he/she responded with care and concern? "I am *so* sorry this is happening to you. I want you to know that I care for you and I'm going to be here for you." What if your friend listened with attentiveness and reassured you about his/her concern?

What might you be **thinking**? ("It really helps to know I have a friend. I'm glad I had him/her to talk to.")

_____

_____

_____

_____

What might you be **feeling**? (Ex: relieved, comforted, cared for?)

_____

_____

_____

_____

What might your **behavior** look like? ("I'd probably be able to get back to work—I'd be more focused." Or, "I'd hug my friend and go home to love on my kids.")

_____

_____

_____

_____

_____

_____

What **intimacy needs** were met by your friend?

_____

_____

_____

_____

When our needs are met, we would likely see a more positive outcome:

Needs Met ▶ Truthful Thinking ▶ Positive Emotions ▶
Productive Behavior

The following chart illustrates what how most people respond to a pattern of met or unmet needs:

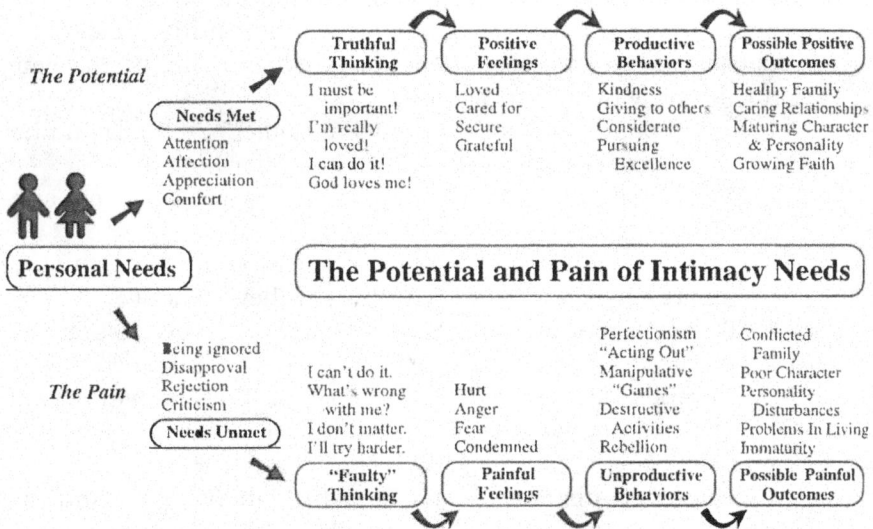

	Truthful Thinking	Positive Feelings	Productive Behaviors	Possible Positive Outcomes
The Potential	I must be important!	Loved	Kindness	Healthy Family
Needs Met	I'm really loved!	Cared for	Giving to others	Caring Relationships
Attention	I can do it!	Secure	Considerate	Maturing Character
Affection	God loves me!	Grateful	Pursuing	& Personality
Appreciation			Excellence	Growing Faith
Comfort				

Personal Needs

The Potential and Pain of Intimacy Needs

			Perfectionism	Conflicted
	Being ignored		"Acting Out"	Family
	Disapproval	I can't do it.	Manipulative	Poor Character
The Pain	Rejection	What's wrong	"Games"	Personality
	Criticism	with me?	Destructive	Disturbances
Needs Unmet	I don't matter.	Hurt	Activities	Problems In Living
	I'll try harder.	Anger	Rebellion	Immaturity
		Fear		
		Condemned		

"Faulty" Thinking	Painful Feelings	Unproductive Behaviors	Possible Painful Outcomes

Now, let's peek into the lives of two children to see the Needs Principle in action:

Sally is a twelve-year-old who rides the bus home from school each day. Because her Mom is busy with civic responsibilities, community service, and church committees, Sally usually comes home to an empty house. Her Dad works sixty-to seventy-hour weeks trying to get ahead, and on weekends has to have "his" time for TV, golf, and other sporting events. Sally struggles with making friends and feels lonely dealing with peer pressure. She longs for Dad's verbalized love and praise. She wishes Mom would have time for some "girl talk" or just window-shopping with her at the mall.

A sixteen-year-old boy begins paying attention to Sally, calling the house, and driving her home. Her parents are concerned that she is too young and the boy is too old. Sally resists breaking off the relationship and thus experiences her first of many "groundings" as angry outbursts fill the air at home. She spends more time withdrawn in her room, hurting alone. It's not long until she is sneaking out at night. She begins lying about her activities and friends.

When Sally's needs are not met at home, both Sally and her parents become vulnerable to that downward spiral:

Needs Unmet — attention, approval, respect, affection, support, comfort.

Unhealthy Thinking — "What's wrong with me? I must be unimportant. I don't matter. Nothing will ever change."

Painful Emotions — hurt, bitterness, anxiety, insecurity, loneliness

Unproductive Behaviors —Angry outbursts, withdrawal, lying, manipulative "games," seeking for needs to be met in inappropriate ways.

Painful Outcomes — conflicted relationships, "shutting down" of emotions, moral compromise.

Are we saying that Sally's problems are all her parent's fault? Certainly not! Sally is definitely making unwise (even wrong) choices.

What we are saying is that Sally might not be so vulnerable to those temptations had her parents been more consistently involved with her, meaningfully meeting her needs for attention, affection, support, etc. Sally is responsible for her part—and parents responsible for theirs!

STOP AND CONSIDER

How might the following situation be best understood?

_____

_____

Three-year-old Bobby runs into his daddy's study, proudly clutching his first finger-painting masterpiece.

"Daddy, Daddy! Look what I did today!"

"Not now, Bobby. Can't you see I'm busy?"

The spiral begins...

Possible Unmet Needs:_____

_____

Possible Unhealthy Thinking:_____

_____

Possible Painful Emotions:_____

_____

Possible Unproductive Behaviors:_____

_____

Possible Painful Outcomes:_____

_____

After you have analyzed the possibilities, discuss your responses with your spouse or partner.

"Aren't you being a little hard on Bobby's dad?" you may be asking. "Maybe he had a deadline and just didn't have time right then. It happens! Lighten up on the guy."

We're not lobbying for instant gratification. In fact, learning to delay gratification is an important milestone on a child's journey towards maturity. Assuming Bobby's dad did have a pressing deadline and was unable to give Bobby the attention and approval he needed at that moment, he could still have affirmed the validity of Bobby's need along with expressing a caring commitment to meet it later. Let's look at an alternate route Bobby's dad might have taken:

"Hi, pal! I can see you're really excited about your picture. Tell you what. I need about thirty minutes to finish this report, and then when I'm finished I'll come to your room and you can tell me about your picture and about what you did at school today. Then we'll hang your picture on the refrigerator door so Mommy and baby sister can enjoy it too." He follows that up with a hug and Bobby leaves the room feeling affirmed and loved. What a difference!

Let's reconsider "the case of the soccer-ball-eating tree" to further illustrate how needs which are met positively contribute to desirable outcomes in the lives of our children. Consider ...

Where was the victory? In the retrieved ball? No, a greater blessing between father and son had been experienced that afternoon. Consider the impact upon Eric of:

Needs Met — Attention, support

Healthy Thinking — "I must be important. Dad must really care about me to come out here to get that ball for me even when he was busy. Dad must really love me to want to help me like that!"

Positive Emotions — loved, secure, hopeful, important, grateful, relieved.

Productive Behaviors — As they stood triumphantly in the backyard, Eric threw his arms around David and said a heart-felt, "Thanks, Dad!" That *behavior* of giving appreciation sprang from a grateful heart. Eric had freely received and was prompted to freely give (Matthew 10:8).

Positive Outcomes — Sense of being loved, belonging; ability to develop intimate relationships, maturing personality; attitude of gratefulness.

Parenting with intimacy **means knowing what our children need and then consistently giving to meet these needs!**

Children don't fully comprehend their needs, so it's crucial for parents to understand their child's needs, validate the importance of these needs, and focus on "giving" to meet these needs. It's modeling for our children how we have been loved by Christ—He knows us completely and takes initiative to sacrificially give to meet our needs.

This is important because much of a child's acting-out behavior may be related to unmet needs. Unfortunately, we often concentrate on the wrong or unproductive *behaviors* instead of also exploring their *unmet needs*. We then tend only to *correct* their behavior instead of *also meeting their needs.* Successful parents don't just address inappropriate behaviors—they also consider and try to address unmet needs.

Parenting with intimacy means knowing what our children need and then consistently giving to meet these needs!

It's not "either-or." It can and should be "both-and!" It's not that we only seek to meet underlying unmet needs and ignore the wrong behaviors. Rather, we seek to do both!

The Zacchaeus Principle

Christ ministered to many individuals across the pages of Scripture. He was particularly sensitive to peoples' **pain**—physical, emotional, and spiritual. He was, to them, the Great Physician. He met people at their point of **need**—physically, spiritually, and relationally. He was to them the Great Provider. Christ accepted and ministered to sinners while not condoning their wrong behavior. Christ demonstrated unconditional love as He viewed a person's **worth** as separate from their **behavior**. *"But God demonstrates His own love toward us [declaring our worth], in that while we were yet sinners Christ died for us"* (Romans 5:8).

Jesus is a perfect model and example of how to minister to an individual's need. Let's consider His strategy with a tax-collector named Zacchaeus and a Samaritan woman at Jacob's well. (Read Luke 19:1-10 and John 4:7-26) In his interaction with these two individuals, He modeled for us the attitude and action we should have and take with our own children.

First, let's consider a first-century tax collector named Zacchaeus:

His Behavior	likely included stealing, deceit, lying
His Feelings	possibly lonely, rejected, guilty, fearful, insecure
His Thoughts	possibly "no one cares"; "nothing will ever change"
His Needs	he probably needed acceptance, security, approval, respect, attention

How did Christ minister to him? *"Zacchaeus, hurry and come down, for today I must stay at your house"* (Luke 19:5) Christ did not attack his behavior—"Zacchaeus get down from there, you lying, cheating thief!"—even though Christ knew all about Zacchaeus and his wrong behavior. Instead, He ministered to his needs for acceptance, attention, security, approval, and respect. Jesus initiated fellowship with this unpopular man and Zacchaeus experienced positive feelings and thoughts which led to changed behavior:

"So he came down at once and welcomed Him gladly," (Luke 19:6).

"Look, Lord! Here and now I give half of my possessions to the poor, and if I have cheated anybody out of anything, I will pay back four times the amount," (Luke 19:8).

Next, let's consider the outcast Samaritan woman:

Her Behavior	adultery, immorality
Her Feelings	possibly guilty, insignificant, outcast, lonely
Her Thoughts	possibly "What's wrong with me?"; "I'm such a failure."
Her Needs	she probably needed attention, acceptance, respect, security, approval

How did Christ minister to her?

"Give me a drink," (John 4:7). He broke social custom by giving her attention!

"Whoever drinks of the water that I shall give...shall never thirst," (John 4:14)—accepting her by offering the gift of Himself unconditionally—before she changed her behavior!

The Samaritan woman must have experienced a life-changing encounter because, *"Many of the Samaritans believed in Him because of the word of the woman who testified"* (John 4:39).

Parenting with intimacy requires looking beyond others' faults and seeing their needs!

"Accept one another, then just as Christ accepted you," (Romans 15:7)

Acceptance doesn't mean condoning sin but rather looking beyond sin to see need—just as Christ looked beyond our sin and saw our need. God has declared the truth that we all sin, and He has also taken the initiative to meet our need for redemption by sacrificing His Son to die for us.

Will you allow the inexpressible joy and wonder of that truth to so work in your life that it prompts and empowers changed behavior in you? (*"The love of Christ constrains us."*) As it does, others will look to you as a good steward of this amazing grace! And nowhere is this stewardship of grace more needed than within your own families.

Apply the principles

Reflect on Christ's ministry to Zacchaeus and the Samaritan woman. Reflect on the faults Christ has *"looked beyond"* in your life and then express your gratefulness to Him:

Lord, I'm impressed with the way you looked beyond Zacchaeus' behavior and met his needs. I'm also touched with the way you looked beyond the behavior of the woman at the well.

This is significant to me because you've looked beyond my faults. You've looked beyond my...

_____

_____

_____

_____

For instance, (*"God I am amazed at how you were able to look beyond the lies, deceit and dishonesty of Zacchaeus. It's hard to believe you were able to look beyond the Samaritan woman's sinful lifestyle. You loved these people in spite of their behavior. This is significant to me because you've looked beyond my apathy, my lack of responsibility, selfishness and pride. And you still chose to die for me."*)

Scripture tells us that Christ accepts us; He loves us with an everlasting love, and we can be put into right standing with God through a relationship with His Son (Romans 15:7; Jeremiah 31:3; II Corinthians 5:21). In other words, He looks beyond our faults and meets our needs. When we have behaved inappropriately or have sinned, we need Christ's acceptance. We need His welcoming arms. Christ loves us and wants a relationship with us in spite of our flaws, imperfections and sinful behavior. His acceptance is unconditional, His favor is unmerited, His love freely given! It's our gratitude for such love which prompts changed behavior in us, just like Zacchaeus!

What feelings do you have about the truth of Christ's unconditional acceptance? Share your feelings with God. Tell God about the impact of His acceptance in a prayer to Him now.

_____
_____
_____
_____

For example: (If you feel grateful, thankful, overwhelmed, blessed, cared for, loved, you might pray something like:) *God, I feel grateful that You don't focus only on my behavior. You love me and want a relationship with me in spite of my actions.*

Close your prayer with these thoughts: *"God, you promised in the book of James to give me wisdom (James 1:5). Please give me the wisdom to see the needs beneath my child's deeds. Help me to show my children the same acceptance You have shown to me. I want to give what I have received from you."*

Scripture Reflection & Prayer of Thanksgiving — 1 Peter 4:10

"Each one should use whatever gift he has received to serve others, faithfully administering God's grace in various forms."

You have reflected on the "manifold" (many-sided) nature of God's grace as He lovingly extends His affection, comfort, acceptance, and forgiveness to us. Now, consider how as parents He wants us to be "good stewards" in sharing this many-sided grace with each of our children. Write a prayer of thanksgiving for how God has blessed you and then mention to God specific aspects of His grace you want to share with each child. (For instance: *"God, I want to show Peter the same forgiveness that You have shown me. You don't remind me of all the times I've messed up. I want to give him that gift as well."* Or, *"God, thank You for the way You accepted me. While I was still a sinner, You gave Your Son to die for me. When Melissa and I dis-*

agree about privileges, help me to show her acceptance that's not based on her behavior.') Write your prayer here:

———————————————————————————————
———————————————————————————————
———————————————————————————————
———————————————————————————————
———————————————————————————————
———————————————————————————————

As you seek to look beyond your children's faults and see their relational needs, have your antennae up and your eyes and ears open. Opportunities to minister to their needs may come when you least expect them.

Special Thoughts for Single Parents

As a single parent, discuss your children's wrong or unproductive behavior with your partner. Talk together about whether certain needs may be going unmet. Having these discussions will help remove your aloneness and regain perspective. Your partner can give you insight into how you're responding to your child's neediness. Brainstorm together about how to "meet the need beneath the deed."

Special Thoughts for Blended Families

The relationships between adults and children can be so emotionally charged that trying to identify needs may seem overwhelming. Particularly in blended families, it will be important to allow your partner to help you see beyond a child's behavior. Together as adults, discuss behavior and possible needs that may be going unmet. Then decide who should work to meet these needs and how that might take place.

Experiencing Biblical Truth

"Accept one another then, just as Christ accepted you," (Romans 15:7).

1. Think about a recent time when you "blew it"—when your own behavior was unproductive, unhealthy, inappropriate, or sinful. Reflect on any times you may have been: selfish, insensitive, disrespectful, verbally or harsh or abusive, unfaithful, disloyal, rejecting, unforgiving, unsupportive, inattentive, unloving, critical, impatient, or withdrawn. Briefly describe your behavior and the circumstances:

_____

_____

_____

_____

(For example: *I was harsh and impatient with the kids on Friday—the day my boss criticized me in front of the rest of our staff.*)

2. Describe what you were thinking and feeling during those circumstances. Write about your thoughts and feelings here:

_____

_____

_____

(For example: *I was feeling embarrassed, and angry. I had invested a great deal of time and energy preparing my report. His criticisms were about my style, not about quality or accuracy. I then felt angry at the kids that they couldn't take care of themselves.*)

3. Which of your intimacy needs may have gone unmet? Write your ideas here: *"I was probably needing . . .*

_____

_____

(For example: *I was needing **respect** and **appreciation** from my boss. I needed **comfort** after it happened.*)

4. What feelings do you have about Christ's unconditional acceptance of you in spite of your behavior? Considering your behavior, how does it feel to know that Christ sees and cares about your unmet needs, not just your deeds?

*"I feel . . .*_____

*because*_____

_____

(For example: "*I feel grateful because He knows me and He cares about me anyway. I feel relieved because of His acceptance.*")

5. Earlier in this chapter, you identified a connection between your child's needs and his deeds. Do you remember any occasion when you focused only on your child's deeds and missed an opportunity to meet relational needs? Write any recollections here:

I recall a time when . . . _____

_____

*and I responded with . . .*_____

_____

*My child probably really needed . . .*_____

_____

(For example: *I recall a time when Brandon was whining and complaining. I responded with anger, raising my voice and threatening to discipline him. When that didn't work, I started ignoring him. He probably really needed my comfort and attention. I missed his need and just focused on getting him to stop the whining and complaining.*)

6. Share one of these missed opportunities with your partner. Be sure to include how you feel about those missed opportunities. (For example: *I regret not being able to see past Brandon's behavior. He was needing my attention, but received being condemned and left alone instead.*)

Homework for Our Homes

Try this with your children:

1. Tell your children a story about your own growing up—about a time when your behavior got you in trouble. Make sure, however, to identify an unmet need that was connected with your deed. (For instance, *"I remember the time when I was being picked on by one of the kids in my class. I told my teacher, hoping that she'd have some kind words to say to me. I needed comfort from my teacher. Instead, I got mean words and a lecture instead. I was so sad, hurt and angry that it was very hard to do what I knew was right. I picked a fight with the boy on the playground that day. I got in trouble both at school and at home."*)

2. Give this brief summary as you end your story: *"Sometimes when we are needing kind words, a hug or special attention and no one gives to us, we feel sad, hurt and mad inside. When we're feeling this way, it's especially hard to do what we know is right. It's important to do what's right—and, it's OK to tell someone what you need, too."*

3. Then ask: *"Can you remember a time when you've felt sad or mad and it was hard for you to do what was right?"* Wait for their responses. Talk with them about what needs may have been unmet: *"You shouldn't have hit your brother. And, I also wonder if you might have been needing a little more of my attention that day?"*

4. As you interact with your children this week, pay close attention to times when they misbehave. Look at the situation or context of the misbehavior especially with any recurring misbehaviors. What might they be feeling? What might they be thinking? What need(s) may have been unmet? Write your thoughts and reflections here:

Situation: _____

_____

_____

Misbehavior: _____

_____

_____

Child's possible thoughts and feelings:_____

_____

_____

Child's possible unmet need(s):_____

_____

_____

What you might do to meet the need: _____

_____

_____

5. Discuss the above with your spouse or partner sometime before continuing to the next chapter or class session.

Chapter 3

——— ■ ———

GOD'S PLAN FOR GROWING UP
(KNOWING YOUR CHILD'S TEMPERAMENT AND DEVELOPMENT)

You've barely pulled away from the driveway and the incessant clamor from the back seat begins. "Are we there yet?" "How much farther?" "When will we get there?" "She's touching me!" "He's bothering me!" "Tell her to stop looking at me!" "She's on my side. Tell her to move!" Sound familiar?

Interestingly enough, kids aren't the only ones asking, "Are we there yet?" Beleaguered parents often echo this same sentiment as they search for the energy to press on. Fueled by America's belief that faster equals better, we're to the point that a three-minute wait for the microwave to deliver a completely cooked meal seems tortuously long! And, if faster is better, instant must be best!

Nothing could be farther from the truth when it comes to rearing our children. Growing up is a long, slow process. Yes, there are bursts of change and rapid development from time to time, but for the most part, we're involved in an 18 to 20 year process, or more!

As is true of our attitude toward so much of what God has put here for us to enjoy and appreciate, we tend to devalue childhood in our society. We tell our kids with our words and actions to "Hurry and grow up." The underlying message is that their importance is found in what they will become—*when* they finish school, *when* they get their degree, *when* they get a good-paying job, *when* they marry the right person, *when* they have a family of their own. There's a Greek word that defines this attitude—*hogwash*! They are important *NOW*—not when. And we can learn to enjoy and celebrate the long process of growing up, appreciating the intricate, sometimes amazing dimensions of God's design for the journey.

God has created and ordained the process of growing up. Gaining an understanding of the orderly progression of the stages God has preordained for our children to pass through enables us to be more empathetic and equips us to help them discover their uniqueness and God-given potential. It's not enough, though, just to **know** *about* kids in general. We must *specifically* **know our kids** and help them know themselves. This can only happen within the confines of loving relationships. God's plan is for a child to grow up in an environment rich in relationships, not merely information.

In order for a child to grow up as God intends, this equation must be in place:

ROLES plus RELATIONSHIPS equals GROWTH!

Healthy children grow up in the context of relationships in which each person fulfills their proper role. This means adults must be willing to be adults who are free enough from their own childhood and self interests to respond like adults. Kids are not asked to shoulder adult responsibilities, and moms and dads don't act like children. Dads are dads. Moms are moms. Kids are kids.

The plan includes two important aspects: God's design of your child's temperament and His plan for your child's developmental growth.

Parents must be willing to fulfill many roles as their child grows toward adulthood. In this chapter, you'll be challenged to look at your role as "guide". How have you assisted your child through the various stages of God's timetable? How have you communicated acceptance during each of these stages? The developmental milestones or watershed events that must occur at various ages along God's appointed timetable are extremely important. Nobody ever grew up to be a healthy, mature adult by avoiding them. If children don't deal with the issues of being twelve when they are twelve, they will have to deal with them later—at twenty, twenty-five, thirty-five, forty-five.

In order for us to effectively "guide" our children, we must continue the process of "unwrapping our gifts." Chapter 1 focused on discovering our children's unique priority of intimacy needs and how to meet them. In chapter 2 we considered the powerful impact of needs—met and unmet—and how important it is for parents to appropriately respond to our children's needs. In this chapter we'll be focusing on God's purposeful plan for growing up and how each child "follows" this plan. This plan includes two important aspects: God's design of your child's temperament and His plan for your child's developmental growth.

Particularly as we consider your children at each stage of development, a word of caution...well, actually two words of caution: NO SPEEDING! Even though your child may have already grown through several of these stages, don't hurry through those pages in this book. Thoughtfully consider each developmental stage, because they build on one another. And, in case you need further motivation to take your time, we'll be asking you to do some soul-searching and reflection for each stage. So, slow down and enjoy the trip.

"Designer Genes"
Your Child's Temperament

Your child's "growing up" began long before his or her eyes first beheld the glaring lights of the delivery room. Psalm 139 offers a beautiful confirmation of the fact that God was actively at work not only while baby was in the womb but even before conception.

> *For Thou didst form my inward parts; Thou didst weave me in my mother's womb. I will give thanks to Thee, for I am fearfully and wonderfully made;*

Wonderful are Thy works, And my soul knows it very well. My frame was not hidden from Thee, when I was made in secret, And skillfully wrought in the depths of the earth. Thine eyes have seen my unformed substance; And in Thy book they were all written, the days that were ordained for me, When as yet there was not one of them. (Psalm 139:13-16)

God loves variety. Blond hair, blue eyes. Brown hair, brown eyes. Red hair, green eyes. Tall, short, and in between. "Red and yellow, black and white...They are precious in His sight." These verses from Psalm 139 assure us that we were each created by the Master Designer, according to plan—no miscalculations, no mistakes. In a sense, we all made our grand entrance into this world wearing Designer genes!

These "Designer genes" determine more than just our physical characteristics. Temperament is, for the most part, genetically determined as well. Webster defines temperament as "the characteristic physiological and emotional state of an individual, which tends to condition his responses to the various situations of life." In other words, it's how we're "wired."

Some kids, by temperament, are extremely **adaptable**. Very laid back. No matter what happens, it just kind of rolls off. Change is no big deal. But there are also those kids who go to pieces over a slight variation in their routine. Change sends them into a tailspin that often results in a crash landing.

Another temperament characteristic is **rhythmicity**. This has nothing to do with whether they'll be the next Ginger Rogers or Fred Astaire. It's how their day-to-day internal biological cycles are set. Rhythmicity determines the regularity of a child's hunger/feeding schedule or how easily a child falls into a consistent, predictable schedule. Rhythmicity also includes the predictability of a child's sleep-wake cycle. For instance, some babies sleep calmly all night and are awake all day. Others sleep all day and are awake all night. These patterns tend to stay with a person throughout life. That's why some people are "morning people" and others are "night people."

A child's **activity level** is another example of temperament. Some kids seem to have minds, mouths, and "motors" that move constantly. Others tend to lean more toward being couch potatoes.

A fourth temperament characteristic is **intensity of reaction**. This tells us how much energy is used when a child expresses emotion. With some children, if we were to graph their display of emotion it would be relatively "flat line"—only subtle differences of emotion could be detected. Other children express their feelings with great intensity. Everyone is aware of their emotional highs and lows. These kids' line graph would look like the Grand Canyon, with plenty of peaks and valleys.

Approach or withdrawal describes how a child may tend to respond to something new, such as new food, a new toy, a new person, or a new environment. Some children seem to want to "attack" life. Presented with something new, they plunge right in and maybe are somewhat bored with sameness. As babies, they smiled and "cooed" with new people. Other kids take more time with new things; they tend to withdraw or pull back in the face of new stimuli. They may have cried the first time grandma attempted to hold them.

These perspectives regarding temperament illustrate the complexity of every human being and thus how important it is for us as parents to **know our children!**

Let's say Johnny comes into this world with the temperament characteristic of high **activity level**. He seems to be awake and moving most of the day. If parents have observed this characteristic from birth, we would suggest that Johnny's constant movement as a toddler may be indicating aspects of his divine genetic formation.

Now, we're not implying that Johnny be allowed to damage property or get into things that might hurt him, all because "that's just the way he is." Temperament characteristics may be contributing to Johnny's high activity, but these characteristics don't give parents license to permit Johnny to misbehave.

What we are saying is that it may be a greater challenge to parent highly active Johnny. We're also saying that Johnny's activity shouldn't automatically be labeled "sin" or automatically disciplined in the attempt to try to get him to stop being so active. It would be a bit like trying to get a red-haired kid to stop being red-haired!

Thus, we'd suggest the following goals for Johnny's parents in order to help Johnny experience God's abundant and unconditional love through his parents and also to help Johnny develop some inner self-control:

1. **Accept Johnny's high activity level unconditionally**; in fact, even strive to celebrate it as a part of how God likely designed Johnny. Meet Johnny's intimacy need for acceptance (Romans 15:7). Do this by giving him many and various ways to safely be active, and be active with him by playing active games, running with him, and cheering for him as he runs around.

2. **Work with Johnny lovingly, patiently, and prayerfully**, beginning early and continuing through his childhood to help him develop inner self-control—one of the "fruit of the Holy Spirit" (Galatians 5:22).

While parents can mold, shape, direct and discipline (see Chapter 7 for more detail), they cannot change a child's God-given design. And yet, some parents attempt to do just that. Sometimes their efforts are subtle—withholding attention or affection from the "bad kid." Other attempts may be as blatant as saying, "Why can't you be more like Sarah? She always sits quietly and never says a word." Or, "Why can't you be more like Billy? He takes naps like he's supposed to and he knows how to sit still. Why do you have to be moving all the time?"

This "Why can't you be more like _____" message leaves children vulnerable to discouraging, condemning thoughts such as, "There must be something wrong with me." or "Why does Mommy like Billy more than me?" or "Why bother. I can't do anything right." The child's needs for acceptance, approval and respect are left unmet, leaving him/her vulnerable to feelings of hurt, rejection, anger, or discouragement.

Applying the Principles

What temperament characteristics have you observed from early in their lives? Assess your children according to their temperament characteristics. Write their "scores" in the appropriate blank. Then consider: what might your temperament characteristics be? Assess yourself!

1. High Activity..Low Activity

    1   2   3   4   5   6   7   8   9   10

Child's score:_____ Child's score:_____ Child's score:_____ My score:_____

2. Low Adaptability...High Adaptability

    1   2   3   4   5   6   7   8   9   10

Child's score:_____ Child's score:_____ Child's score:_____ My score:_____

3. Difficult to Schedule/Unpredictable.....Easy to Schedule/Predictable

    1   2   3   4   5   6   7   8   9   10

Child's score:_____ Child's score:_____ Child's score:_____ My score:_____

4. Very Intense   Low Intensity of
Expression of Feelings..Expression of Feelings

    1   2   3   4   5   6   7   8   9   10

Child's score:_____ Child's score:_____ Child's score:_____ My score:_____

5. Withdraw   Approach
From New Things / People...New Things / People

    1   2   3   4   5   6   7   8   9   10

Child's score:_____ Child's score:_____ Child's score:_____ My score:_____

STOP AND CONSIDER

Which of your children seem at times "easier" for you to parent?_____
At times more difficult for you to parent?_____
_____

Now, look at your temperament assessment for your "easy" child. Do you see a high score? Write your reflections here:___
_____
_____
_____
_____

Now, look at the temperament assessment for your "more difficult" child. Do you see a lower score? Write your reflections here:_____
_____
_____
_____
_____

Now look at your temperament assessment of yourself. Is there any correlation between "who is most or least like you" and which child you find easiest to parent? Any correlation between "who is most or least like you" and which child you find most difficult? If so, why? _____
_____
_____
_____
_____
_____

Paradoxically, the child we find most difficult to parent may be either the child that is most like us or, our "difficult" child might be most unlike us, depending upon how we feel about that child's particular characteristics or tendencies.

For instance, a less active child may be easier for most parents, but if we place a high value on being active, the less active kid may present a problem to us. It depends upon how we view that characteristic.

Consider that an outgoing, gregarious parent may tend to get along well with the outgoing gregarious child, but a shy, withdrawing parent may conflict with that same child. Yet if the parent struggles with feeling bad about being so shy, that parent may have conflicts with a child who is also shy because that parent doesn't like that about himself.

Or a parent may have conflict with a child who scores low on adaptability. That child may be viewed as inflexible or excessively rigid because the parent loves change and variety.

We're suggesting that we consider these issues here because there may be clues about why we may be experiencing tension or conflict with one or more of our children. These perspectives may also serve to alert us to tendencies to "favor" one child over others.

Romans 15:7 says to *accept one another just as Christ has accepted us.* How might the need for acceptance be related to the issues above? How might your challenges in parenting be related to your child's need for acceptance of his or her temperament qualities? Write your thoughts here (For example: *"I find myself being intolerant and impatient with Matt. I love change and find it easy to adjust to changes in routine. Matt's whole world is disturbed if we decide to leave for a basketball game 10 minutes earlier. I need to accept his adaptability level as different than my own and display more patience with him. Christ accepted me unconditionally. I need to show Matt the same acceptance."):*

_____

_____

_____

Sadly, relationships are often overshadowed by harsh strokes of black and white, reduced to sets of rules and regulations and standards of conformity. If we're not careful, our message to our children may be: "To be different from me is to be wrong, even flawed."

Certainly rules and standards and conformity have their place in the parenting process, but saving them for shaping of Christ-like behaviors and attitudes will be more productive. Intimate relationships are characterized by the acceptance of individual differences, valuing another's uniqueness and honoring personal preferences, while at the same time encouraging Christ-likeness in accordance with His Word.

Ephesians 2:10 says, *"For we are His workmanship, created in Christ Jesus for good works, which God prepared beforehand, that we should walk in them."* The word *workmanship* translates a Greek word that means poetry. We are God's "poetry." He has made each child unique, exactly as He wanted. Follow His lead. Rather than trying to change God's rhythm and rhyme, develop an appreciation and acceptance for the "poem" He has entrusted to your care. As you put your hand in your children's and guide them in painting their life's landscape, use the vast array of colors God has made available to you. Each child is a masterpiece in the making, revealed one brush stroke at a time.

STOP AND CONSIDER

Stop and reflect on the truth expressed in Ephesians 2:10. Your child is God's poetry—a product of His creativity and craftsmanship. Write a prayer to God, asking Him to show you the special design in each of your children. Ask Him to give you an "admirer's perspective." Ask God to give you the perspective of one who is admiring a great work of art or creative masterpiece. As you reflect on the stages of growing up, pray that God will allow you to appreciate the beauty of His precious gift—your child!

For example: *"God please help me to appreciate the unique way in which you have created Bethany and Brittany. You have created them just the way You wanted. They are two of Your very special masterpieces. Help me to see them that way—as precious poems. They have intricate features of personality that you designed. Please give me an "admirer's perspective" as I live with them each day. Amen."*

_____

_____

_____

_____

_____

Thus far in this chapter we have examined in-born, God-designed temperament qualities—their "Designer genes." **Now let's consider the implications of what happens as a child grows through the predictable stages of human development**—the physical, mental, and emotional changes which God has planned for growing up.

We'll look at each stage and what we need to know in order to effectively "guide" our children, helping them accomplish what's important in each stage.

Who Do You Trust? Or Do You?

(Infancy: Newborn to 18 months)

In the not-so-distant past, it was thought that newborns just needed to be held, fed, burped, changed, and put to bed. It was believed that for infants, not much learning was taking place, not much was happening in their world.

We have since learned that infancy is an incredibly active time of growth and development. Amazing things are happening!

Most importantly, moment by moment, hour by hour, day by day, this infant is learning a fundamental lesson that will determine the quality of the foundation upon which all future relationships are built. As baby's intimacy needs are either met by caring adults or remain unmet, the question is answered, "Can relationships be trusted?" It's not a matter of *whether* they will learn about trust but *what* will they learn.

It is not a matter of *whether* they will learn about trust but *what* will they learn.

If we could get inside a newborn's thought processes, we might hear something like this: "When I'm hungry, my mommy feeds me. Daddy does too sometimes. They hold me. They change me when I'm wet. They talk to me and sing to me. Daddy lets me pull his whiskers. When I cry they come to see what's wrong. They rock me and pat me on the back. I can trust Mommy and Daddy to love me and take care of me."

We see the flip side of this all around us in daily news reports. A growing number of babies are learning quite the opposite lesson about trust. Instead of having their needs met by loving, caring adults, they are neglected, abandoned, or abused. Inside *this* infant's head we might hear, "When I'm hungry no one comes. When I cry because I'm wet, I'm punished. When I need to be comforted, I'm ignored. The world is an unsafe place. Since I can't trust anyone else to meet my needs, I'll do whatever I have to do to meet them myself—and it may be at your expense." A destructive mind-set is developed that will greatly hinder the child's ability to cultivate intimate relationships throughout life.

There is no more crucial lesson for growing up than learning to trust. An inability to trust impacts not only the child's horizontal relationships with other human beings, but also their vertical relationship with God. It's difficult to trust a loving Heavenly Father if you haven't been able to trust your earthly care givers.

That's not to say all is lost if our parenting in this first stage was deficient. There is always hope. God's grace covers a multitude of tough situations. Through His grace and provision, we can allow God to include us in His plan for meeting needs now which may have been missed in this stage. As we have come to experience God's trustworthiness and have received His provision, we are able to demonstrate that trustworthiness to others. We can become an earthly channel for God's consistent care.

See Appendix A on page 241 for further discussion and application for this developmental stage.

Learning to Balance the Teeter-totter
(Toddler: Walking—36 months)

One small step for toddler, one giant step for the rest of the household! The day a child learns to walk, life is forever changed. A whole new world opens up to children as they make the amazing, liberating discovery that they have two legs that will carry them almost anywhere they want to go.

> Holding on and letting go. Mommy and Daddy help balance this process by providing limits and controlling the consequences of the toddler's choices.

From the outset, let's renounce the label, "The Terrible Twos." This has become a popular description for this age group because of parental frustration. Undeniably, developing an intimate relationship with a toddler can be trying—maybe even exasperating, but this label implies that two-year-olds are somehow a mistake in God's plan. Imagine how one's perspective might be altered if we referred to this age as "The Terrific Twos." It really is, you know. Toddlers are accomplishing a very difficult, horizon-expanding task. They are learning to balance autonomy and dependency.

It might help to understand this process if you visualized a teeter-totter. On one side is *dependency* ("How long do I stay attached to Mommy and Daddy, depending on them for every-thing?"). On the other side is *autonomy* ("I let go of Mommy and Daddy, begin to be responsible for myself and my own choic-es."). Achieving this balance is a lifelong endeavor, but it begins in earnest at this age.

Everything about this stage boils down to a process of *hold-ing on* (dependency) and *letting go* (autonomy).

- ◆ *Learning to walk* — Pulling up on the coffee table, holding on for balance, and then letting go and taking off as fast and as far as little legs will cooperate.
- ◆ *Learning to talk* — Holding on to their tongue muscles, their ideas, and the wind in their lungs—and then letting loose to the delight of adoring adults.
- ◆ *Potty training* — You get the picture!
- ◆ *Power struggles* — Holding on to and letting go of opinions and will.
- ◆ *Personality* — One moment they're in Mommy's arms with a sweet, cherub-like smile, telling her with words and actions "I love you." Thirty seconds later they're down on the floor stomping their feet and saying, "No!"

Holding on and letting go. Exasperating at times, but nor-mal! That's not to say there's no place for limits at this age. Mommy and Daddy help balance this process by providing lim-its and controlling the consequences of the toddler's choices.

How can we help toddlers navigate safe passage through this stage?

The most important thing we can do for them is help them experience unconditional love through words and actions: "I'm not going to let you run into the street. I'm not going to let you throw a ten-minute temper tantrum. By the same token, I'm not going to put you in a playpen with a box of animal crackers and expect you to be quiet all day. I am committed to doing whatever is in your best interest."

Avoid messages to the child such as, "If you loved me, you'd take a nap like I asked you to." Or, "If you loved me, you would-n't get mad when I have to tell you 'no'." Or. "If you loved me, you'd never do anything wrong—you'd be perfect." These messages imply that children are under constant pressure to "perform"—to prove their love to their parents!

Unconditional love communicates, "Not only do I love you, but because I love you I want to "enter your toddler world." I understand that it's hard for you to hear the word 'no', because you're just now learning to balance appropriate autonomy with dependency. But remember, I'm striving to say and do what is truly in your best interest, even when you don't understand it."

Consistent experience of unconditional love helps the toddler resolve the "Good Parent/Bad Parent" dilemma. If we could get inside a toddler's thoughts, it would go something like this: "Good Mommy brings me my blanket and gives me a snack. She loves me, and I love her. Bad Mommy makes me take a nap when I don't want to and won't let me have a cookie before dinner. She must not love me, and I don't love her. Good Daddy wrestles with me on the floor and reads me a bedtime story. He loves me, and I love him. Bad Daddy tells me no when I try to get the goldfish out of its bowl and won't let me pull the dog's tail. He must not love me, and I don't love him."

If a child has consistently experienced unconditional love in action, he or she will have integrated the "two mommies" and "two daddies" and will begin to perceive that, "The mommy who feeds me, plays with me, and cuddles me is the same mommy who sometimes tells me 'no' and doesn't let me do everything I want. She loves me, and I love her. The daddy who carries me on his shoulders and pulls me in my wagon is the same daddy who sometimes gets concerned about what I've done wrong and puts me in time-out. He loves me, and I love him. It's *because* they love me that they discipline me. Their rules and consequences protect me and are for my good, even if I don't like them."

Resolution of this dilemma is crucial for the sound development of a child's concept of God: "The same God who loves me also disciplines me. He sees my mistakes and loves me anyway. Just because He does things that I don't like doesn't mean He doesn't love me. Just because I don't understand how He is loving me now, I still believe that He loves me and is doing good in my life."

See Appendix A on page 243 for further discussion and application for this developmental stage.

Discovering A New World
(Early Childhood—3-5 years)

Many writers have described these as "The Magic Years." Although historians have ascribed the title of "Discoverer of the New World" to Christopher Columbus, let it be declared henceforth and forevermore that children in these early childhood years are making great discoveries about their world on a daily basis. Life is an adventure! Everything is new and exciting. Curiosity may have killed the cat, but it's the lifeblood of children in this stage. Each new discovery helps them grow in several key areas:

Physically

Kids in this stage love to demonstrate how strong they are—flexing what they consider to be their powerful muscles to convince any doubters. They need a safe place to run, jump, and climb, not only for the necessary physical exercise it gives their growing bodies, but also because it allows them to make daily discoveries about what they can do physically.

Part of this discovery process is their fascination with body parts. They begin to ask lots of questions. Much to the consternation of red-faced parents, these questions are often blurted out in the most embarrassing places—like the grocery store aisle or the check-out lane—and are never in a whispered voice. Although mortifying to parents, these questions are sincere and innocent—and deserve simple, concrete answers. Save the "Everything You Need to Know" version for later. Little Kid 101 will suffice for now.

They're great imitators too. If you give a three- or four-year-old a football after he's watched a game on TV, he'll take it into the yard and run back and forth shouting signals to his imaginary teammates, convinced he's the world's greatest, strongest, and fastest football player. He has no idea (and does-n't care) what the rules or objectives of the game are.

This penchant for imitating behavior is one of the dangers of watching TV, because they have no concept of the danger of much of what they're watching. Sammy ended up in the hospital after trying to leap off the roof of his house. During the ambulance ride, Sammy looked at the paramedic and lamented, "But it looked so easy when Superman did it!"

Mentally

Parents could retire by age forty if they had a dollar for every time their preschooler asked, "Why?"

> *"Why is the sky blue?"* *"Because God made it that way."* *"Why?"*
>
> *"Why do I have to take a nap?"* *"Because your body needs the rest."* *"Why?"*
>
> *"Why can't Daddy stay home today?"* *"He has to go to work."* *"Why?"*

Although it can grate on parental nerves, this God-given curiosity and sense of "I wonder why" is a tool to help them learn to cope with the world around them. Two-year-olds didn't worry about the rest of the world; they coped by assuming they were the center of the universe. Three-year-olds make the discovery they're not and are trying to understand their giant world. How do they do that? How do you help them?

You could try the lecture circuit. "Sit down. I need to tell you a few things in order for you to make your way in this world. First of all, you should never, ever steal things because it breaks statute 305.42 and a policeman might arrest you if you get caught." You could try this approach, but your success rate would be zilch. God didn't design kids this age to learn about the world around them simply through facts, lectures, and information. This is hard for a generation obsessed with the Information Super-Highway to swallow! Facts play a part, but God has given us a greater opportunity to teach kids about their world through deepening an intimate relationship. What does this look like at this age?

God has gifted them to be able to learn about the world they live in through fantasy and their imagination. They must be able to balance this fantasy and imagination with reality, but they'll need help to accomplish this task. Guess who gets to help!—Mom, Dad, and other caring adults. Recognize their need to fantasize as well as their need to deal in reality.

Sometimes in our striving (albeit well-meaning striving!) to be perfect parents, we tend to go to one of two extremes. On one end are very permissive parents who say, "I want my child to be creative, un-stifled, uninhibited. I want him to be able to explore everything, do everything, fantasize about everything." They set no limits—ever. That approach will eventually drive the parent crazy and is unhealthy for the child as well. On the other side, there are parents who say, "My child is going to live in the real world. Forget fantasy. Get real, kid! Straighten up. That fantasy stuff is a waste of time, and it's all of the devil anyway." This approach is equally unproductive. The goal is balance. Easier said than done, but here are some suggestions to get you started.

First, read to your child...read to your child...read to your child. God has enabled them to learn about the world through storytelling and imagination. Reading affords marvelous opportunities for teaching preschoolers about their world and the biblical values they'll need to be successful. Reading offers such opportunities because you're capitalizing on a preschooler's developmental strengths. Sit down with them and read a story—a Bible story or a favorite book. They'll soak it up, and you'll have a captive audience.

Second, play with your child...play with your child...play with your child. You can teach your child any lesson you want by getting down on their level and playing with them. Sadly, playing is a lost art for most Americans. For a lot of reasons, we're all too busy with the "important" things in life to have time to play with our kids. Television is stealing this opportunity away from us not only because of the quality of programming available but because it's such a readily-accessible babysitter. Kids often spend more time interacting with the tube than they do with their parents. And, as odd as this may sound, toys can hinder quality play time. There are some incredible toys available to kids these days—if parents could just afford the batteries. However, many of these toys are so elaborate that they do everything for the child, leaving nothing to the imagination. Parents, if we're honest, we often buy these toys for ourselves and then get our feelings hurt when our kids aren't interested in playing with them beyond Christmas morning.

Gender Identity: What it means to be a boy or girl

Kids this age are also discovering what it means to be a boy or girl. There are several key times of life for a child to develop a sense of maleness and femaleness, and this is one of them.

For instance, it's not uncommon for a three-and-a-half year old boy to say things like:

> *"Mommy, I want to sit next to you in the car."*
> *"Mommy, can we play a game together?"*
> *"Daddy, get lost! I'm with Mommy now."*
> *"I want Mommy to put me to bed."*
> *"Mommy, I'm going to marry you."*

Young boys want to attach to their mommies. It's normal. And dads hate it! Paul threw his professional training out the window when it came to Matthew's desire to be with Vicky. Coming home after a long day of helping kids and their families learn how to relate more intimately with one another, Paul was primed for his little boy to jump into his outstretched arms as soon as he came through the back door and bestow upon him the title of World's Best Dad. Nothing doing! Matthew wanted to be with Mommy. Paul Warren, highly trained behavioral pediatrician, responded like any other normal dad—his feelings were hurt: *"Vicky, can't you make him....?"*

Towards the end of this stage, though, this little guy begins to notice that the strongest relationship in the family seems to be between Mommy and Daddy: *"Mommy loves me, but she and Daddy have something super special."* So by the time he's four-and-a-half or five his thinking begins to change. Now he says, *"You know what? It's OK to be a boy. I want to grow up to be just like my daddy, and someday when I grow up I'll marry a lady just like my mommy."* (Moms, this same process goes on between dads and daughters as well.)

Empathy

Empathy for children this age means, "I no longer believe that I'm the center of the universe." It's the opposite of entitlement (the belief that "Everything should be the way I want it to be. Everyone else should agree with me. I should always be able to get my way."). They can and should begin to discover that other people have feelings, desires, and opinions that are different from theirs and that others' feelings, desires, and opinions should be respected.

Help your children begin to develop a "feeling vocabulary." Talk about feelings as you see sadness, anger, frustration, and fear. Helping them learn to identify these feelings first in themselves will help them recognize them in others. (See Chapter 6 for more detail.)

Another avenue for modeling empathetic respect for others is for us as adults to be willing to apologize and request forgiveness. As you attach value to their feelings and opinions by acknowledging when you have hurt them, it sets an example for them to follow.

See Appendix A on page 245 for further discussion and application for this developmental stage.

Developing Character and Competency
(Middle and Late Childhood—6-11 years)

Theorists used to call this stage "latency" because it was thought nothing much was happening or going on inside the child. What a misnomer! These kids are busy learning how to deal productively with their world both within and outside the family. They need to establish their identities in terms of who God says they are—His infinitely valuable and beloved children as well as developing Christ-like character qualities. And, they are discovering and exploring new interests and developing competencies physically, mentally, and emotionally.

> They need parents who genuinely know them and who are committed to lovingly meeting their needs in ways that fit this stage of development. And this is also an important time for other adults to be part of our children's growing up journey.

Our children cannot accomplish any of these crucial aspects of growing up alone. They need parents who genuinely know them and who are committed to lovingly meeting their needs in ways that fit this stage of development. And this is also an important time for other adults to be part of our children's growing up journey.

Several issues significantly affect our children's progress through this stage. We will address the importance of how we handle competition and our children's need for achievement. We will also consider the challenges and opportunities presented by sibling rivalry and the battle over "fairness."

Competition

Adults who brag that their children's programs are competition-free are deluding themselves. Where there are kids this age, there's competition. Healthy competition gives kids the opportunity to identify and develop their strengths and work on their weaknesses. With proper support they can learn how to solve problems.

How do we know we have "healthy" competition? Three parameters must exist:

1. **Adult involvement.** If you've ever spent time with a group of kids this age when they're out on the playground, you know that it takes about five minutes before somebody's complaining, "He cheated!...It's not fair!...You're stupid!" An adult needs to be available to "referee" and help get things settled. The key is for the adult to not "over-control," forgetting who the activity is really for.
2. **The opportunity to both win and to lose.** This may sound heartless, but "healthy" competition affords both the opportunity to win and lose. What better time to learn how to handle defeat and disappointment as well as victory than while under the protective umbrella of a loving, supportive home environment!
3. **The experience of being part of a team.** This is of particular importance in this "Me" generation that says that the most important things in life are personal freedom and self-sufficiency. "I don't need anybody. I can pull myself up. I don't need any help." This attitude isn't biblical. The Bible emphasizes loving one another, serving one another, working and living together. A team experience—whether it's sports, clubs, church groups, or other civic groups—gives kids the opportunity to experience interdependency and support—that we as people need each other (I Corinthians 12:21; Ecclesiastes 4:9-12).

Achievement

Kids this age need to experience the approval of their achievements in at least three arenas.

1. **They must see themselves as approved in the eyes of their parents.** A word of caution here. This does not mean that their worth is based on what they do. This is a delicate balance, as precarious as walking a tightrope. This may be more challenging for some parents. If your child isn't a great student, is a klutz on the ball field, can't draw, can't sing, can't play an instrument, and isn't the cutest kid in school, you're going to have to dig a little deeper. But keep digging! Keep in mind, this pursuit is not so you can look good but so your child can experience a sense of affirmation and approval from you. Jesus heard from His Father "You are my beloved son/daughter in whom I am well-pleased!" just before He went out into the desert to be tested by the Devil. In the same way our children need to experience a blessing for who they are, as well as how proud we are of anything they accomplish or put forth effort to achieve. Approving of their character strengths, such as their caring, politeness, helpfulness, patience, is an important aspect of meeting this need.

2. **They must see themselves as successful at something in the eyes of their peers.** Case in point: Remember those horrible rainy days you used to dread back in grade school? You couldn't go out at recess so they'd take you to this dark, dingy room they called a gym. The teacher, desperate for a break, would just leave you in the room with these parting instructions (which fell with the weight of a death sentence on some shoulders), "OK, you kids play basketball. Johnny and Susie, you two will be the captains. Choose your teams, and I'll see you in about fifteen minutes." And so the agony begins. The really cool kids are drafted first; the mediocre kids go in the second, third, and fourth rounds. Then the two captains hem and haw around for what seems like an eternity because they don't really want any of the remaining prospects. Peer rejection cuts deeply, the wounds heal slowly.

   One pro-active parental step in this regard can be cultivating family friends with positive peer influences. We may not be able to alleviate the rejection of peers at school or scouts or team events, but we can cultivate relationships with families who have children that are more accepting.

Don't leave your child to travel this peer journey alone. Get involved and look for other people and families who can be meaningfully and lovingly involved. Taking initiative now to develop positive family relationships with healthy peer relationships will pay many dividends as your children enter adolescence.

Another thing parents can do is allowing children to explore various interests (sports, music, dance, art, etc.) to look for and cultivate something at which the child can excel. Beware of overdoing it—perhaps one or two involvements at a time outside of school is probably enough for most kids.

3. **They must see themselves as successful in the eyes of adults other than their parents.** Think back to when you were this age. Did you have significant other adult besides your parents? Was it a teacher? A coach? A Scout master? A Sunday School teacher? A grandparent or favorite aunt or uncle? If you had someone, their approval, support, and encouragement spurred you on to take a few risks and reach for goals that you might otherwise have viewed as unattainable.

Sibling Rivalry

One of the most frequently asked questions at our seminars is, "What can I do about sibling rivalry?" Most parents consider sibling conflict to be a scourge from God meted out as punishment for their past sins ("What goes around comes around!").

Sibling rivalry (perhaps better termed "sibling competition") is not always the evil nemesis we've made it out to be. Lots of brothers and sisters who fight are also close and share good times together. And sometimes a little competition between siblings can appropriately spur an older sibling to not let himself be "out-done" by younger brother.

However, sometimes sibling rivalry runs amuck when kids are getting seriously hurt physically and/or emotionally or when there are very few positive times. When sibling rivalry falls into the "run amuck" category, it's usually not a sibling problem—it's a parent problem. In these instances, one or more of three underlying factors are usually present:

1. **One or both parents may be consistently favoring one of the kids.** Emphasis here is on "consistently" because every day in your home there's probably one of your kids you don't like very much—one who's on "your bad side." That's just part of growing up in a family. However, destructive sibling rivalry will usually develop when one or both parents consistently favor one of the children. We ought to be very careful of any tendencies we may have to do this by working on the suggestions in this workbook relative to meeting the needs consistently of each of our children.

2. **There are unresolved problems in the parents' marriage.** Kids are incredible barometers of their parents' marriage, and when the marriage is perceived as going downhill kids will start fighting. It's as though they're entreating their parents, "Whoa, Mom...Dad...Deflect a little of that tension and anger in our direction! Don't fight with each other...referee our fights instead."

3. **One of the parents, usually Dad, is too involved outside the home.** In order to get Dad back home, the kids will act as ornery as they need to in order to get his attention and bring him back home. "Yoo-hoo, Dad! This calls for your touch. You're the only one who can handle us. Better come on home."

Destructive sibling rivalry can leave deep wounds and drive families apart. If you see this in your family, first try to address one of the three common underlying contributors above. *Especially consider seeking to deepen your marriage intimacy through a class or small group. (See suggestions for marriage intimacy resources listed at the end of this workbook.)*

The Battle Over Fairness

By this age, parents have heard the complaint "It's not fair!" ad nauseam. Most parents' standard reply? "Whoever said life was fair?! Why, when I was your age..." This reply may seem satisfying as it rolls off the tongue, but it evaporates immediately upon hitting the air. It does nothing to reassure a child that you care about them or their feelings—OK, life isn't fair. So now what? What do I hold on to?

Fairness, at least the way kids this age measure it (in microns!), is impossible. If things were *fair*, the chocolate cake would have to be divided exactly, not one crumb more or less. In order to be *fair*, your nine-year-old would have to go to bed at the same time as your one-year-old. After all, that's the only *fair* way. But then, of course, a cry of "But that's not fair!" would fill the room; and round and round you'd go.

Suppose your ten year old son wants to have a mass sleepover with 12 friends so that they can go out in the middle of the night to "toilet paper" some houses. You discuss it with your spouse or friend and you bravely determine that the sleep-over is OK but not the late night activity. Unfortunately, your son has already promised his buddies that they'll be able to do it. He then hits you with a relentless stream of *"It's not fair!!!"*

Arguing and trying to explain why your way really is right and not unfair is as ineffective and as probably as painful as beating your head against a brick wall. The higher road takes the approach that says, "This is not an issue of fairness. It's an issue of trust. I know it's doesn't seem fair, and I understand you're upset. You're going to have to trust me; this is the way it needs to be."

See Appendix A on page 247 for further discussion and application for this developmental stage.

Change, Change, Change!
(Adolescence: 11-18 years)

Stepping Away (Early Adolescence: Ages 11-13)

Early adolescence begins for most kids around the age of 11 and continues for about three years. Some incredibly exciting things are happening for these kids as they cease being little boys and little girls and start becoming young men and women. In fact, these years are perhaps the most important of all.

Research tells us, and clinical experience bears it out, that people who have serious psychological difficulties later in life (in their thirties and forties) most often made their decision about the worthwhileness of life during early adolescence. These kids desperately need parents and other adults who will enter their world and walk through this time with them.

Most people think this is the age when puberty (what an ugly word!) begins, but it actually begins at age five or six with gradual, ever-so-minimal hormonal changes. (Quick, grab the smelling salts. Mom just fainted!) A massive explosion occurs around age 11. Girls take the lead, usually beginning at about nine-and-a-half or ten. They experience their growth spurt early in puberty and then begin their menstrual periods toward the end. Boys begin later, around age ten-and-a-half to eleven, and are the exact opposite. Their sex hormones begin to flow in early puberty, and their growth spurt kicks in at the end (much to their chagrin!).

The important thing about sexuality in early adolescents is that **at no other time is maleness and femaleness more different than during this stage.** Boys are incredibly physical. They're curious about what things look and feel like. Romance? Forget it! Girls, on the other hand, are all romance. Knights on white horses. "Ooooh. He may call me tonight. He's soooo dreamy." Physical? Forget it! And so, wherever you have hordes of young adolescent boys and girls together, you'll find the boys whispering and chuckling, chasing and teasing the girls, looking for opportunities to touch them. While the girls are screaming, "Stop it! Stop it!", underneath they're cooing, "I love it. Maybe he'll call me tonight and we'll fall in love."

Two messages for parents here. One is to understand that this is normal. You can't get to healthy adulthood without going through these adolescent years. Do you want them acting like adolescents now, or when they're thirty? Take your choice. Second, there's a strong message here regarding dating. Kids this age going on one-on-one unsupervised dates is a disaster waiting to happen. Their interests are so totally divergent—boys all physical, girls all romance—that they'll be horribly uncomfortable. They're thinking, "Is this all there is to a relationship? No thanks."

Their thoughts and feelings are undergoing some major transformations as well. First, they have an attack of aphasia. This is a fancy medical term meaning...they don't talk...at least not to parents. So, you have these kinds of "conversations:"

> *"What did you do in school today?"*
> *"Nothin'."*
> *"What did you have for lunch?"*
> *"Don't remember."*
> *"What would you like to do tonight?"*
> *"I don't know."*

This is exasperating to parents because the perception is that they're intentionally withholding information just to be irritating. Actually, their thoughts and feelings are so new and so overwhelming that they couldn't find words to express them even if they understood them—which they don't!

They can also be incredibly disorganized. If you need proof, look in their notebooks and you'll find papers stashed every which way. Math papers in the English folder, love notes in the science folder and there's that three-month-old permission slip that never made it home. Contrary to the opinion of the adults in their lives, their disorganization doesn't stem from laziness or willful carelessness. Life is suddenly so incredibly different and overwhelming they just can't keep up the pace. It's amazing how many kids who were previously well-organized and successful students hit adolescence and are now "out-to-lunch."

What do they need from adults? They don't need to be put down or shot out of the saddle—they don't need *"What's wrong with you? Are you ever going to get yourself organized?"* That just reinforces exactly what they're fearing about themselves: *"I may never get organized. I may never get out of this."* They need both empathy and structure.

These kids are also experiencing "ambivalence"—extreme contradictory feelings—for the first time. Ambivalence looks something like this: "The same people that I really love sometimes make me so mad that I feel like I hate them." They discover that the things in life that are really scary are also pretty exciting. For months before starting junior high or middle school they hear the horror stories about kids getting lost and how kids in the hall appear from nowhere and beat you up and try to flush your head down the toilet. On the one hand, they're scared to death. On the other, they can't wait. They can't imagine anything more exciting.

> These kids are also experiencing íambivalenceîóextreme contradictory feelingsó for the first time. íThe same people that I really love sometimes make me so mad that I feel like I hate them.î

Separation and individuation become major issues. These big words simply mean moving away from parents and becoming more of the person God has created them to be. Hopefully, this process has been taking place in small increments from day one, but it bursts onto the scene full steam ahead at this age. We wish we could tell you it will be resolved soon, but for some it's not resolved until thirty-five...thirty-nine...forty-three...!

At the same time all this is going on, **these kids are also making the horrifying discovery that the parents they've depended on for everything for so long are, after all, imperfect.** The same parents who were once thought to have all the answers now seem to know nothing. How can this be? It must be that these are not the real parents. There must be perfect parents out there somewhere. Many kids who are not adopted begin to wonder if they really are adopted. Maybe they were switched in the hospital nursery and that their real parents are out there somewhere looking for them. Adopted kids may become convinced that their biological parents are the perfect parents and long to locate them. Children of divorce may assume that the parent who doesn't live with them is the perfect parent.

Sadly, at a time when kids need adults the most, this is the age that adults often avoid their children like the plague, leaving them very alone. In most churches, it's easy to recruit adults who love working with the older youth or who gravitate to the younger kids because they're cute and fun. But when it comes to 11 to 13 year-old kids—"Sorry, I served my time." What an opportunity awaits the adult who's willing to roll up their sleeves and get involved! These kids don't need head-wagging nay-sayers, they need adults who are available to provide attention, acceptance, approval, comfort, and support.

See Appendix A on page 249 for further discussion and application for this developmental stage.

Bold New Steps
(Middle Adolescence: Ages 14—16)

Having survived early adolescence with a scrapbook full of memories that might best be described as "The Agony and the Ecstasy," our heroes now embark on the second leg of their adolescent journey somewhere around fourteen. They'll be on this road for about three years.

They're now capable of some one-on-one relationships. Their commitment to those relationships, however, vacillates from day to day.

Whereas they have previously depended on their peer group *as a group,* **they're now capable of some one-on-one relationships.** Their commitment to those relationships, however, vacillates from day to day. One day they're best friends. They're going to grow up together, go to college together, go into business together. Best friends forever. Inseparable. Two weeks later, "I can't stand that person. I don't ever want to see him again." Two weeks later...fused at the hip again. Up and down. It's a normal part of growing up, but they need adults in their life to help establish sound limits and appropriate expectations.

They are also wrestling with the issue of *ego-centricity* (self-centeredness). The first way this manifests itself is that they make the assumption that the world is their stage and they're performing for an adoring audience. If you need proof, take a trip to a large amusement park. You'll see groups of kids this age climbing the rails, screaming and yelling at people 500 yards away, assuming everybody wants to know they're there. Paradoxically, at this age something we affectionately refer to as "the zit principle" kicks in. That is, they assume that all people see are their negative characteristics. Case in point: Debbie was a straight-A student until she was required to take a speech class and received a resounding F. She steadfastly refused to get up and give a speech simply because there was a small pimple on the tip of her nose. Although it was so microscopic one would have to strain to see it from a foot away, she was convinced that all eyes would be riveted on her zit. She would rather take an F than risk being the class joke and be humiliated beyond recovery.

Adolescents' ego-centricity is also evident in their powerful feeling of uniqueness. This comes out in two ways. One is they know everything, and they are the only ones who know everything—parents know nothing. But, while they know lots of facts and understand the tragic consequences of drugs, premarital sex, smoking, and drinking, their sense of uniqueness causes them to believe that those things only happen to other people, not to them. They also assume that because their thoughts and feelings are so new to them that they must be new to everyone else as well. So conversations similar to this one begin to occur. Your sixteen-year-old daughter retorts, "But, Mom, you just don't understand. You've never been in love before." She's not trying to be argumentative. She actually believes it!

Incredibly idealistic, they may go for the highest of what is good...but they're also enticed by the highest of the highs and the lowest of the lows. That's one reason why certain music can be dangerous. Drugs, obviously, are dangerous because they feed off this love of experiencing new ranges of feelings. As Christian parents, we must be careful not to present a relationship with Jesus Christ only as "getting high on Jesus." That will appeal to them at this developmental phase, but what happens when they reach a low point in their life? If they associate Jesus Christ only with the "highs," they will begin to flounder in their faith. They need a more complete picture, a firmer foundation upon which to build.

Sexuality, much like their hormonal curve, could be graphically depicted by a roller coaster...ups and downs...incredibly high then latent, incredibly high then latent. Consequently, these kids do not belong on one-on-one car dates with nothing to do. Leaving home with the best of intentions, their hormone curve kicks into high gear and you suddenly have two teenagers in a car with time on their hands and nothing to do. In other words, you have trouble.

But these kids also don't need adults in their lives who think their generation has gone to the dogs. They need adults who remember what it was like to be a teenager. Like their predecessors, they need lots of understanding and empathy. Redeem the time. Their years at home are rapidly coming to an end.

See Appendix A on page 251 for further discussion and application for this developmental stage.

Spend some time expressing the above to God, asking and experiencing His forgiveness as necessary. And consider talking to your child about this as well, maybe even confessing and seeking your child's forgiveness.

The Final Leg
(Late Adolescence: Ages 17- ?)

The final leg of the adolescent journey begins at around age seventeen and ends by twenty-one . . . twenty-five . . . thirty . . . forty . . . They are now ready for relationships that are characterized not by the up and down curve but by intimacy. Not sexual intimacy, not marriage . . . but a decision to have relationships characterized by a commitment to the other person and the other person's best interests rather than on self-gratification.

Relationships characterized by a commitment to knowing each other and genuine giving in order to care about another.

This is similar to the goal they had back in their toddler days—balancing the teeter-totter of autonomy and dependency. They've now achieved *autonomy with attachment.* "I will be responsible for myself. I'm not going to ask or expect someone else to be responsible for my feelings and my behavior (*autonomy*). But I realize I can't, and don't want to be, a lone ranger so I'll also be committed to caring involvement with other people and relationships (*attachment*)."

By the time adolescence is over, they will have finally resolved the storm that began when they were eleven or twelve and discovered their parents were not perfect. Adolescence is not truly over until this issue is successfully resolved. People fall into three different camps in their attempts to do this.

> By the time adolescence is over, they will have finally resolved the storm that began when they were eleven or twelve and discovered their parents were not per-

First is the group who continue year after year to rage against their parents. "I can't believe the mistakes my parents made. I'm never going to get over this. They really messed up and messed me up in the process. I'm so mad at them."

The second group takes a totally opposite stance. "My parents were the most perfect parents who ever lived on the face of the earth. They never made any mistakes." Impossible! Imperfect people are destined to make mistakes.

Then there's the group in the middle. "Yes, my parents were not perfect. I wish my dad had not done some of the things he did, and I wish my mom had done more. But, you know what, I've worked through that—I've let myself feel and express my pain and I've received others' comforting care. And I have forgiven them, come to love them more, and I'm now ready to move on with my life. God expects me to be responsible for being a good steward of the life He's given me."

The first group puts their parents on trial and never lets them off the witness stand. In their self-appointed position of raging prosecutor, they allow no opportunity for forgiveness. The second group goes to the opposite extreme, choosing instead to deny the truth, assuming that this is how they obey the biblical command to "honor your father and mother." The group in the middle experience the blessing of mourning and comfort (Matthew 5:4) and offer and find forgiveness (Ephesians 4:31-32): "My mom and dad made mistakes. They were imperfect parents, just as I'm imperfect." They've discovered that truly honoring your father and mother means being committed to the truth. Only then can one truly finish growing up. *"You shall know the truth, and the truth shall make you free"* (John 8:32), free to serve others in love (Galatians 5:13-14).

See Appendix A on page 253 for further discussion and application for this developmental stage.

God has a beautiful plan for growing up. Take time to enjoy every stage. Allow your kids to enjoy each day and to feel your approval for who they are right now.

Special Thoughts for Single Parents

After determining your child's developmental stage, identify her outstanding intimacy need(s). Make a simple plan to meet some of these needs—one way to meet one need, for starters. Focus on what you *can* do and then involve other adults if needed. For example, you may not be able to build castles with your five-year-old every day, but you can give attention by reading bedtime stories. Your adolescent will appreciate your support when you take fifteen minutes to call her after school just to see how her friends responded to her new glasses.

Some of the relational opportunities may be impossible for you to meet yourself—such as male companionship if you're a single mom, or female companionship if you're a single dad. Become pro-active. Expand your "family of choice" to include other adults who might meet these needs. You might establish relationships with church groups, community groups, or partnerships with intact families.

Special Thoughts for Blended Families

The response to divorce and remarriage will be different according to a child's age and development. Children may be very expressive about their loss, verbalizing their unsettled or hostile feelings. Their grief may also reveal itself in more subtle ways. They may show signs of regression—bed-wetting or thumb-sucking—or display poor performance in school. Teens are most likely to demonstrate their grief through acting-out behaviors. Seize every opportunity to express comfort: *"I'm sure you must be confused and upset at times—and I just want you to know that I care."*

Consider how each of your children responds to the divorce and remarriage. How has each child dealt with his loss? Have you disciplined acting-out behavior but still maintained an atmosphere of openness? Have you provided opportunities for each child to share her concerns about the absent parent? The new living arrangements? The new step-parent? The new siblings? Tell each child you want to hear concerns and then follow through to make time to do so.

Experiencing Biblical Truth

"Rejoice with those who rejoice . . ." (Romans 12:15)

1. As you reflect on each child's complete journey, what special memories come to mind? How has God blessed you through the gift of your children? Write about one of your favorite parenting memories here—one that makes you feel happy or joyful as you recall it: *One of my favorite parenting memories is . . .*

_____

_____

_____

_____

   For example: *When I think about Tiffany's difficult birth and early complications, I can't help but be grateful for the first day she walked, the time she won the first place ribbon in the track meet and the times I get to see her play tennis. God has given me a child who has a faith greater than my own. She never says, "I can't."*

2. Partners, share this positive memory with each other. Romans 12:15 directs us to *"Rejoice with those who rejoice."* Celebrate with one another. Rejoicing might sound like, *"Wow, I'm so happy for you!"* or *"That's terrific! I'm really glad you had that special experience."*

3. Now, reflect on your own childhood journey. Think back to your own years of growing up. What positive memories do you have about your childhood? Each of you choose one positive memory and share that with your partner and rejoice with one another. *My positive memory from childhood is . . .*

_____

_____

_____

_____

4. How did it feel to share these two positive experiences with a partner and have him/her rejoice with you? Write your responses here:

(For example: *"I felt cared for when my partner listened to me and then celebrated with me."* or *"I felt connected. I had never heard my partner share that experience before."*)

_____

_____

_____

_____

_____

Homework for Our Homes

1. **Plan to demonstrate acceptance to each child this week.** Surprise your son or daughter with words like, "I just want you to know—I love you just the way you are." or "I'm glad I get to be your Mom/Dad." You might even find a few of your child's baby pictures and reminisce out loud: "I remember thinking that you were the most wonderful child in the world, and I still do." or "You were God's special gift to our family—I still see how special you are."

2. **When your child "blows it," makes a mistake or disobeys this week, be especially sure to communicate acceptance.** Your words might sound like, "I'm glad I'm your Dad even when you mess up." Or "I love you even when you disobey." Let your child know that your love and acceptance is unconditional—just as Christ has accepted you (Romans 15:7).

3. **Go back through the chapter and select one practical idea from one of the "Stop and Consider" or "Applying the Principle" boxes.** Talk with your spouse or journey-mate partner about it. If it looks to be a good idea, try it this week!

Chapter 4

—— ∎ ——

FREEDOM TO BE A PARENT
(DEALING WITH OUR OWN "GROWING UP")

WEIGH STATION AHEAD: PREPARE TO STOP! We've all seen the sign as we've barreled down the highway. Unless you happen to be a truck driver, you've no doubt dismissed it as not applicable to you and kept on going. Not this time. We're all pulling off to "weigh in." What we're likely to find is that we're hauling some extra poundage and need to lighten our load.

It's crystal clear throughout Scripture that God is a God of order in every facet of His creation, including marriage and family. The first biblical reference to marriage is found in Genesis 2:24, *"For this cause a man shall leave his father and his mother, and shall cleave to his wife; and they shall become one flesh."* Genesis 4 then records Adam and Eve bringing forth children and beginning their parenting journey. That's God's order: *leave* father and mother; *cleave* unto one another; *become one* (intimate with one another—physically, emotionally, and spiritually); THEN we're ready to be parents.

As we pull into the weigh station, we may find ourselves faced with a dilemma—we've reversed the order! We're already parents, but we haven't yet finished leaving our family of origin. Unresolved issues from our own growing up experiences may be impacting our freedom to develop intimate relationships with our children.

For instance, as parents we are challenged to give our children attention by entering into their "worlds," but what if our parents were too busy to enter into our worlds? What if the only person who really knew you was the baby-sitter? Every day after school you'd sit and talk to her while she ironed and cooked dinner. She was the only one who ever really listened to you.

Similarly, our children appropriately need approval, but if we never received it then we may be unsure how to give it. Or we may not know what appreciation looks or sounds like. Perhaps when we're called upon to comfort our children through the inevitable disappointments of life, we may feel inadequate to comfort because, as we were growing up, we hurt alone. We will tend to find it difficult to give to our children what we did not receive.

Some of us simply have the tendency to still look to our parents as the main people to meet our needs, rather than trusting God to work through our spouses. We may feel an excessive obligation to gain our parents' approval, so we continue to do whatever we can to make sure they are happy. Our marriages suffer with our parenting also being hindered.

Remember: "leaving mother and father" is not simply a matter of economic or geographical separation. It means we've "left" faulty ways of thinking, unproductive behavior patterns, and unhealed emotions from our growing up. It means we are free to truly honor our parents and other care givers, gratefully celebrating what we did receive from them. It means that we are free to know and love our children as God intends, out of the committed security of an intimate marriage!

STOP AND CONSIDER

Has your "leaving" of father and mother been completed? Did this fully occur before having children? Write your thoughts here.

_____

_____

What feelings do you have about your response?

_____

_____

Think now about a second issue. Can you see ways in which your own experiences growing up have impacted your ability to parent? In what ways?

_____

_____

_____

Reflect on this statement: *It's often difficult to give to your children what you did not receive.* What thoughts and feelings do you have about this statement?

_____

_____

_____

For the most part, David and Teresa Ferguson had been in agreement on how to raise their two daughters, Terri and Robin. However, an interesting dynamic kicked in when their son, Eric, came along. They became divided in their approach to parenting. David found it very hard, if not impossible, to say "no" to Eric. But, not to worry, Teresa was there to pick up the slack! Her motto was "*Nip it in the bud.*" The more she nipped, the more David slacked off, feeling sorry for "poor Eric." The more David slacked off, the more Teresa nipped. They became increasingly polarized in their parenting. David admits that in spite of his "having several academic degrees in this area," it took him awhile to figure out what was going on. It all came into focus one Saturday morning.

The Case of the Lone Begonia

Spring had sprung at the Fergusons'. It was time to get out into the yard and get things cleaned up. Teresa, lover of the great outdoors, was in her glory. David, lover of the great indoors, was not. Everyone had an assigned task and went about their business. Ten-year-old Eric was assigned to the dead plant detail in the front yard. He was to dig up the plants that had died over the winter. Simple, direct, manageable. After some time had passed, David decided to go around to the front to see how Eric was coming along. His findings? One dug-up begonia, one shovel, one missing bike—one missing Eric! Let's let David tell it from here.

"It never occurred to me to go find him, bring him back, and discipline him. I actually walked over, picked up the shovel, and began to dig up the rest of those dead plants. Instead of thinking about what would be an appropriate consequence for his behavior, I'm thinking, 'I'd better hurry up and finish digging up these plants before Teresa catches me doing it!' I had enough training to know this is pathological! I was enabling Eric's irresponsibility and trying to do it as quickly as possible before I got caught."

Asking the Lord for wisdom, David gained insight into the dynamics of what was taking place. His over-permissiveness with Eric hadn't surfaced with Terri or Robin because it was related to a father-son issue from David's own growing up experience.. There was a fear within David that went something like this: "No matter what, I don't want my son feeling about me some of the things at times I felt about my dad growing up. As Eric is growing up, I want him to like me." Because of his own unresolved issues from childhood, David had concluded somewhere along the way that this meant he couldn't tell Eric "no" or set any limits with him.

David determined in his heart that he had to talk to Eric. He confessed to him that he had hurt him by enabling his irresponsibility. He actually apologized to him and asked for his forgiveness. He apologized to Teresa for his lack of support, and together they explored David's growing-up pain. In the days that followed David began to be more strict with Eric and to use that much-feared "no" word, even though it was still extremely hard.

About a month after their conversation, Eric was late getting up one morning and was running around the house trying to get ready for school. Unable to find his own toothpaste, he rushed into David's bathroom, squeezed some of David's toothpaste onto his brush, and was about to walk off, leaving the toothpaste on the counter with the cap still off. David summoned every bit of strength and faith he had as he said, "Buddy, you need to come back and put up the toothpaste." That may not sound like a big deal, but it was for David because of his fear that Eric wouldn't like him.

Eric came back, replaced the cap and, never one to be at a loss for words, looked back at his dad with an impish grin and said, "Dad, I still like you!"

STOP AND CONSIDER

After reading this story, do you have any additional thoughts about your childhood experiences affecting your ability to parent? Like David, have you found that your own unresolved issues at times may impact the way you relate to your children? Write about those here:

_____

_____

_____

_____

So how do we genuinely "leave father and mother" in order to gain freedom to effectively parent with intimacy? How do we fully experience resolution of our past so that we might truly give to our children what they need?

The hurt, the fear, the circumstances will vary; but most of us at times have been hindered in our parenting by unresolved childhood issues. A three-fold process is involved:

1. Face the inevitable emotions—both the joys and the sorrows.
2. Express both the joys and the sorrows.
3. Receive joy and comfort from others.

Let's first look at how to face our emotions:

Face the Emotions

Although we don't know you, according to the Scriptures we are confident we can tell you three things about yourself. As you were growing up:

◆ You had imperfect people around you.
◆ You grew up in an imperfect environment.
◆ You were an imperfect person.

We know, beyond a shadow of a doubt, that these things are true, because you're human. All human beings are imperfect—no exceptions other than the God-man Jesus! A natural consequence of the interaction of these three truths is that you have experienced dimensions of hurt.

Before you are prompted to defend your parents ("My parents did the best they could!"), **let's distinguish between parental *motives* and parental *methods*.** Consider the following diagram:

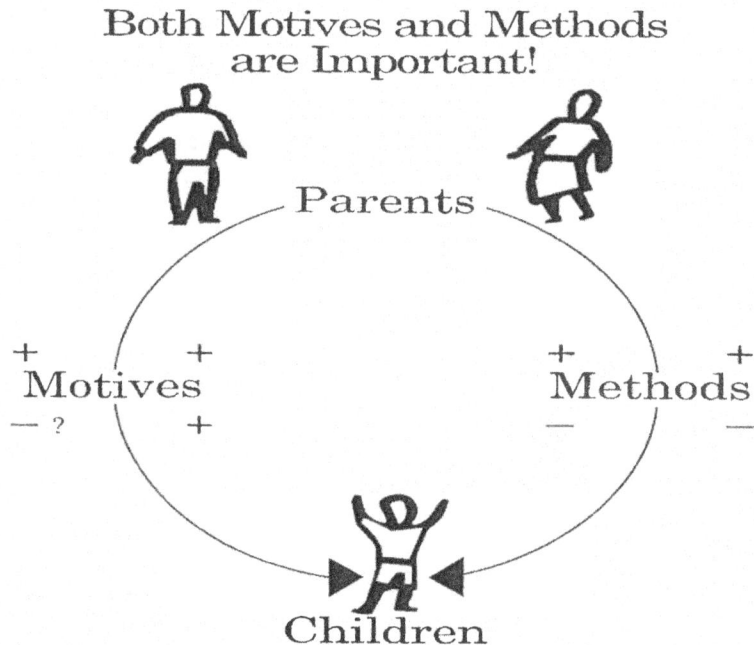

Both Motives and Methods are Important!

Parents

+   +
Motives   Methods
— ?   +   —   —

Children

A parent can have the best motives ("pluses")—*"I love you. I care about you. I want what's best for you"*—but at the same time employ hurtful or unproductive methods ("minuses"). In other words, our parents very likely did the best they could, yet, because they were imperfect, they inevitably at times hurt us. Although they likely did not intend to, it is not possible to grow up pain-free, especially from those closest to us. (And tragically, some parents exhibit both painful methods and painful motives as experiences of abuse or gross neglect would indicate.)

Let's keep in mind: unintentional hurt can still be very painful—if someone accidentally drops a heavy rock on your foot, it still hurts even though the rock was dropped unintentionally.

Also, acknowledging pain does not translate into assigning blame. We must come to see that it involves facing truth about we may have missed growing up and how that may have affected us, especially today.

The Case of the
Imperfectly Made Bed

Like most boys his age, making his bed was not young David Ferguson's top priority. After all, he was going to be crawling right back under those covers in another twelve hours, give or take a few. So, what was the point?

Well, to his Marine drill sergeant father, the point (*motive*) was teaching David responsibility and that a job worth doing was worth doing well. So, at "bed inspection," if the quarter did not bounce high enough off the tightly made bed, the sheets came off and David started over...and over...and over. This sometimes took an hour out of a perfectly good Saturday morning! More importantly, David's need for his father's approval went unmet.

In later years, David and his dad were able to talk about these things and resolve the hurt. As a critical part of a healthy "leaving" process, with great maturity, his dad came to acknowledge that while his motives were good, his methods brought pain. The pain was addressed, healed, and a greatly enriched relationship ensued.

STOP AND CONSIDER

Stop and consider the issue of motives vs. methods: Can you identify ways in which you experienced emotional pain as a child—not as a result of painful motives but of painful methods? (For example, *"I know my mom had to leave me with my grandmother while she went on long business trips. She wanted to provide for me (motive), but I still missed her. When she traveled (method), I felt lonely and unimportant."*)

_____

_____

_____

_____

_____

As previously stated, tragically, many individuals must face the truth that not only were their parents' methods wrong, but their motives were wrong as well. In the case of abuse, incest, and related traumas, both the motive *and* method were terribly wrong. This dual pain of both motives and methods will require additional work to feel and express the deep and profound sadness as well as the comfort of God directly and ministered through the love of other people.

For all of us, the question is not, "Have you experienced hurt?" That's a foregone conclusion. We've all been undernourished in some areas of need, and the result is hurt. Rather, the question is, "Has the hurt been faced? Has it been mourned and comforted?" Facing hurt leads to opportunities for growth. Unwillingness to address pain will tend to hinder our growth as an adult, spouse, and parent.

STOP AND CONSIDER

As we begin this journey into freedom from the past, what thoughts or feelings do you have about beginning the process? Write your perspective below:

When I think about exploring what I might have missed or how I might have been hurt, I ...

_____

_____

_____

_____

Tell God about it. Ask Him to give guidance, peace, healing, and freedom. Write your prayer here:

_____

_____

_____

_____

But why look back?

"It was for freedom that Christ set us free" (Galatians 5:1).

You may be wondering, "Why can't we just 'press on to what lies ahead?'" Questions about whether consideration of our growing up is really necessary may take the following forms:

◆ **What's past is past—why "dredge it up?"** Our response is, we don't want to dredge anything up just for the fun of it; we only want to "dredge up" the past in order to address anything that needs to be healed and resolved.

◆ **"My past is not affecting me."** Our response is, we need to be cautious about assuming this. Do we really believe that it doesn't matter how we were raised? That, for example, parenting doesn't matter? Then why do we have any concern about how we are raising our children?

◆ **"It doesn't matter."** Our response is, often what this resistance really means is that "I don't matter."—That no matter how much I was affected by family influences, I don't have enough value and worth to justify any effort to look at my past. The truth is, you do matter! And if there is something that could be addressed that would help you be freer to give Great Commandment love to your children, then it (and you) are worth it!

◆ **"I don't want to dishonor my parents."** Our response is, our goal is not to dishonor them, but rather to identify truth regarding our relationships with our parents and what we may have received and missed. We are not seeking to blame; rather we are seeking to heal. The Bible does say to honor parents, and we come to honor "real" parents as we admit and forgive their imperfections and receive comfort for our pain.

Although the "events" may be years or decades in the past, the pain of hurt, bitterness, fear, condemnation or shame, and guilt may still be very real—right now in the present. Freedom from the past is what enables us to move forward, intimately relating to our spouse, family and others. As we address what we experienced growing up, we may experience as many as eight growing freedoms:

1. **Freedom to trust God to meet many of our unmet needs** through our spouses or close friends, according to His timetable and agenda.

2. **Freedom to enjoy adult-to-adult relationships with our own parents.** We can be freer to "leave" a dependent, care-receiving role.

3. **Freedom to appreciate the positive qualities in our family of origin relationships.** Unhealed hurts can blind us to positive qualities in our parents or other care-givers. In essence, blockading the hurts can block our awareness of the blessings as well.

4. **Freedom to accept and honor our parents as "real people."**

   "No, I never heard my parents tell me they were proud of me, but it's no big deal."
   "No, I never heard my dad actually say he loved me, but that's just the way he was. It didn't really hurt me."
   "I'm not sure I could honestly say anyone knew me—not really deep-down. But hey, I did ok without it."

This may sound harsh, but these statements just cannot be true. Why? Because each statement indicates significant "aloneness," and God's Word says, "It is not good to be alone," (Genesis 2:18). John 8:32 says, *"You shall know the truth, and the truth shall make you free."* God's Word is truth to be reckoned with; so also is the truth about our growing up. If we're going to find freedom, we're going to have to confront and deal with the truth about your own childhood.

Truly honoring our fathers and mothers means many things, including recognizing the pain that was also present in their lives. This pain may have hindered them in their ability to meet some of our needs. We honor them as we allow them to come down off a pedestal that keeps them out of reach. We honor them as we allow them to be human beings who made (and make!) mistakes. We can only honor "real" people, not "imaginary" ones.

5. **Freedom to be more sensitive to giving to meet our children's needs.**

Until we resolve our own childhood pain, it will be more difficult to give to our own children. If we don't resolve our own pain, we will tend to react in one or the other of two extreme ways: We may be intolerant or insensitive to a child's needs—

"I didn't get a lot of attention, and I'm fine, so why do you need so much?" "When I was upset, they left me to deal with it myself. Didn't hurt me any—why should you need comfort?" Or we may go overboard in our efforts not to repeat our own parents' mistakes. "At all costs, I'm going to give you all the attention I missed, and more!" "Whenever my kid is upset, I'm going to drop whatever I'm doing. No matter what, my kid is going to be comforted!" As well intended as these thoughts may be, they may not represent true giving. The motivation to "do better" may be as much for the parent as it is for the child!

6. **Freedom to avoid the burden of trying to be "perfect parents" ourselves.**

As we saw in Chapter 3, an integral part of every child's developmental journey is coming to grips with the fact that his or her parents were not (and are not) perfect. If we're unwilling to wrestle with that truth and its implications, we're destined to be on a never-ending, unachievable, personal quest to be the "perfect parent." Our children will suffer because of it. For example, without this resolution, we may find it hard to apologize and admit wrong to our children. Children then lose our model of vulnerable confession and asking for forgiveness and thus may not feel the freedom to let us know when they have hurts and disappointments for fear of our reaction.

7. **Freedom to experience the blessing of mourning and being comforted.**

One of the most important benefits of bringing resolution to past pain is God's promised blessing of comfort. Looking back at unmet needs is painful, but these represent losses to be "mourned." Matthew 5:4 promises great blessing that comes to those who mourn as comfort is also received: *"Blessed are those who mourn, for they will be comforted."*

Some people still hurt alone because they're unwilling to express their hurt. Our society, and sometimes even the church presents a subtle message that "It's a sign of weakness to grieve or mourn," or "The more spiritual you become, the less you should feel hurt or loss. If you do, you certainly shouldn't share it."

Yet the Bible declares:

> *"Blessed are those who mourn, for they shall be comforted,"* (Matt. 5:4).
> *"His [Jesus'] power is perfected in weakness,"* (2 Cor. 12:8).

And, if we need more evidence that mourning is all right, Jesus, the God/man, also felt and expressed His hurts and disappointments:

> *"He was despised and rejected by men, a man of sorrows and acquainted with grief,"* (Isaiah 53:3).
> *"My soul is deeply grieved to the point of death,"* (Mark 14:34).
> *"Jesus wept,"* (John 11:35).

If Jesus felt and expressed hurt and sadness, would it be OK for us to do the same?

8. Freedom to resolve any bitterness or unforgiveness.

As pain is comforted, many of us are then freer to make the necessary choice to forgive as we have been forgiven (Ephesians 4:32). Experiencing the care and comfort we may have missed eases our pain so that we can more freely choose to let go of our anger.

STOP AND CONSIDER

Stop and consider the potential freedoms we can experience through facing our hurts from the past. Which of these benefits seem most important to you? Express your thoughts below:

(For instance: *I need to be free from my anger at my father because he seldom gave me attention or comforted me. Whatever it takes, I want to learn how to give true comfort and attention to my children.*)

_____

_____

_____

_____

Tell God about your hope for change. Tell Him your desire to see benefits from looking into your past. Claim the promise of Matthew 5:4—Ask God to bring the blessing of comfort as you mourn. He's a good God who gives good gifts. Thank Him in advance for blessing you in this growing-up journey. Write your prayer here:

_____

_____

_____

(For instance: *"Thank you God for your promise of comfort in Matthew 5:4. There are hurtful things in my past and I know they'll need to be mourned. I pray for the comfort You promised. I also ask that you allow me to see the benefits of looking into my past. I would like to be set free from these painful issues and to be more sensitive to my own children. I do know that You are a good God and desire an abundant life for me. Thank you for the changes You're making in me. Amen.*)

How to Bless Those Who Mourn
Comfort Them!

Sometimes people may hurt alone because spouses or partners might not know how to respond to mourning. Since comfort is so necessary to the healing process, let's consider how to give genuine comfort.

When emotion is expressed (and mourning involves emotions), an emotional response must be given in return—according to Romans 12:15, we are to "*rejoice with those who rejoice, and mourn with those who mourn.*"

But instead, we may offer one of these four unproductive responses: **logic or reasoning, criticism, complaining, or neglect.** These responses are unproductive because they most often do not help relieve sadness or pain. Rather, these responses may actually add to the pain.

Here's how these unproductive responses might sound in a real-life situation. Suppose you've just lost a loved one in death and you're mourning your loss. Others might respond with:

◆ **Logic or reasoning**—"Don't be sad; you know she's better off in heaven," or "It's appointed unto man once to die. Be encouraged; you know you'll see him again!"
◆ **Criticism**—"Don't be so emotional; everyone goes through rough times."
◆ **Complaints**—"I know you're really sad, but I'm devastated! She was one of my best friends!"
◆ **Neglect**—"Say, how's it going at work? I heard your job's pretty tough right now. What's going on?"

STOP AND CONSIDER

Imagine that **you** have just lost a loved one. How would you feel if someone responded to you with one of these statements?

_____

_____

_____

_____

_____

The response to mourning which ministers deep loving care is comfort. **Comfort** includes both verbal and non-verbal responses which convey, *"I'm hurting with and for you in your pain."* Verbalized comfort might sound like:

> *"I can really see you're hurting."*
> *"It saddens me that you are hurting."*
> *"I'm committed to going through this with you."*
> *"I'm sorry you hurt; I hurt for you."*
> *"I want to do whatever I can to help because I care about you."*

Non-verbal comfort might be simply sitting with you—being with you. Perhaps an arm around your shoulder, a hug, a gentle touch. It may well include tears of sadness for you.

Now imagine that someone expresses comfort to you in the midst of your grief. How might you feel?

_____

_____

How might this relate to the promised "blessing" of Matthew 5:4— *"Blessed are those who mourn, for they will be comforted."*

_____

_____

Consider II Corinthians 1:3-4. Whose comfort is being shared? Who is the source of all comfort?

_____

_____

_____

_____

_____

Now, together with your partner, let's continue on our journey of healing past hurts. Keep in mind what you've just learned about comfort. You'll have ample opportunity to both give and receive it.

Identify What Is To Be "Left" Through Mourning and Comfort

You'll never be any more sensitive to others' needs and hurts than you are to your own! So, it's time to put down your reflector shield and conduct an honest self-appraisal.

In Chapter One we identified ten key intimacy needs and asked you to do a "needs assessment" for each of your children. Now the focus is on you. Listed below are those ten needs. With your renewed commitment to facing the truth of your childhood, prioritize a quiet, reflective time to review this list and follow the instructions. You will then share your reflections during an "Experiencing Biblical Truth" exercise at the end of the chapter.

STOP AND CONSIDER

Stop and consider your growing up experiences:

1. Mark the Needs List as follows: If Dad took the initiative to consistently meet the need, put a half-circle (in the space to the left of the need. If Mom took the initiative to consistently meet that need, put the other half-circle) in the space. If you consistently received it from both of them, you'll have a full-circle () in the space beside the need. As you go through the list, you may find some that you missed altogether. Mark those with an X.

Take your time. Try to remember, if possible, a specific time when this need was met, or a specific time when it was unmet. If Mom met your need for acceptance, write down short phrases that describe how she did that. If Dad met your need for attention, write short phrases that tell what that looked like. Try completing the exercises as you remember events associated with your childhood or preteen years. If you can't remember these years, begin with years you do remember—preteen, teen, or young adult.

_____   1. **Acceptance:** Receiving another person willingly and unconditionally, especially when the other's behavior has been imperfect. Being willing to continue loving another in spite of offenses. (Romans 15:7)

_____   2. **Affection:** Expressing care and closeness through physical touch; saying "I love you." (Romans 16:16; Mark 10:16)

_____   3. **Appreciation:** Expressing thanks, praise or commendation. Recognizing accomplishment or effort. (Colossians 3:15b; I Corinthians 11:2)

_____   4. **Approval (Blessing):** Building up or affirming another; affirming both the fact of and the importance of a relationship. (Ephesians 4:29; Mark 1:11)

_____ __5. **Attention:** Conveying appropriate interest, concern, and care; taking thought of another; entering another's "world." (I Corinthians 12:25)

_____ __6. **Comfort:** Responding to a hurting person with words, feelings, and touch; to hurt with and for another's grief or pain. (Romans 12:15b; Matthew 5:4; II Corinthians 1:3-4; John 11:35)

_____ __7. **Encouragement:** Urging another to persist and persevere toward a goal; stimulating toward love and good deeds. (I Thessalonians 5:11; Hebrews 10:24)

_____ 8. **Respect:** Valuing and regarding another highly; treating another as important; honoring another. (Romans 12:10)

_____ 9. **Security (Peace):** Harmony in relationships; freedom from fear or threat of harm. (Romans 12:16,18)

_____ 10. **Support:** Coming alongside and gently helping with a problem or struggle; providing appropriate assistance. (Galatians 6:2)

2. After you've completed this exercise, record your reflections below.

It may be difficult for you to write about your own pain. But avoid "explaining away" or "minimizing" hurt. Just write your feelings—both sorrows and joys. Healing begins at the point of facing truth, both the positive and the painful.

[Ex: *I remember my Dad encouraging me to tackle things I thought were out of my reach and being there to support me. From my dad, I really missed approval. I really needed to know that he was proud of me. Just once, I wish he would have told me what a good job I had done. I remember the times when Mom gave me respect. She was good at giving me "space" and not barging in uninvited. And from my mom, I really missed attention. I needed her to spend time with me, come to my games, and ask about my boyfriend.*]

I remember my dad giving me ...

_____

_____

_____

From my dad, I missed ...

_____

_____

_____

_____

I remember my mom giving me ...

_____

_____

_____

_____

From my mom, I missed ...

_____

_____

_____

_____

3. Identify your emotions, both joys and sorrows.

As you consider what you recorded above, reflect on ways you received from your parents, for which you feel grateful. Record your thoughts and feelings here:

As I consider what I received from my parents, I feel grateful that . . .

_____

_____

_____

_____

Allow yourself also to feel the pain of unmet needs. To grieve is to focus on the emotions associated with your loss, just as you would grieve over the loss of a loved one. Continue writing about your feelings. Can you identify what you felt then or feel right now? *"I felt or I feel ... lonely ... sad ... afraid ... angry ... disappointed ... unloved ... violated ... or unimportant"*

Don't expect to move through this quickly. Grieving is a process, not a once-and-for-all exercise. As experiences and situations arise that again bring the hurt, allow yourself to grieve. Write your reflections and feelings here: Use additional paper if necessary.

I remember wishing ...

_____

_____

_____

and ended up feeling ...

_____

_____

_____

It hurt so much when ...

_____

_____

_____

Express Emotions and
Receive Joy and Comfort

We've taken a significant step of **facing our emotions—both the joys and the sorrows**—through the above reflective journaling. We must now express both the joys and the sorrows and receive joy and comfort from others.

During the "Experiencing Biblical Truth" section at the end of this chapter, we will have the opportunity to share both our joys (gratefulness) and any sadness we may feel with our partners. We will thus also have the opportunity to both give and receive both and comfort.

It may be helpful to specifically share what you need at that time. For instance, *"I have something I'd like to share with you* about some of my needs and feelings from my growing up years. As I do, I just need you to listen and be glad for what I'm grateful for and be sad for what I'm sad about." Or, "I could sure use a hug right now."

Remember, partners, as your partner shares, give undivided attention, eye contact, reassuring touch, and both rejoicing and comforting words as appropriate:

> **"Rejoice with those who rejoice:"** *"I'm so glad for you that you received..."* (Romans 12:15 a.)
> *"I can see where God blessed you with..."*
> **"Mourn with those who mourn:"** *"It really saddens me that you missed..."* (Romans 12:15 b.)
> *"It hurts me that you were hurt like that."*
> *"I'm committed to be here for you."*

Let's also remember that for some of us, **receiving comfort can be quite difficult.** Allow your partner to both rejoice with you and to feel sad about your hurt and to hurt with you. Don't minimize your hurt. It's important to genuinely receive God's comfort through your partner. You might want to verbalize your gratefulness as a testimony of receiving God's comfort. For example, "Thanks for caring," or "Thanks for hurting with me." You might then want to pray together, expressing gratefulness for the blessing of comfort and a partner who cares.

Scripture Journaling and Prayer
II Corinthians 1:3-4

"Blessed be the God and Father of our Lord Jesus Christ, the Father of mercies and God of all comfort; who comforts us in all our affliction so that we may be able to comfort those who are in any affliction with the comfort with which we ourselves are comforted by God."

Take your unmet needs to the great Comforter. Let God know the hurts of your childhood. Let Him know what you missed and how that felt. What do you need from God? Have you been still long enough to hear His loving response? Have you been honest with God about your feelings and experiences? Have you been receptive to His comfort? Will you allow Him to additionally provide His comfort through a partner who cares for you? Write your thoughts or prayers here:

_____

_____

_____

_____

_____

Special Thoughts for Single Parents

As a single parent, in addition to dealing with childhood pain, you will want to mourn the pain you've sustained by becoming a single parent. Individuals who have gone through a divorce or death of a spouse have many grief issues to face. It will be important for you to identify any unresolved losses so that you will be free to respond adequately to your children. With a trusted friend, counselor, or partner work to identify your own feelings, hurts, and losses. Your sensitivity to your own struggles will increase your sensitivity to your children. If you minimize your own pain, you will tend to minimize the hurts of your child. If you get stuck in your own pain and don't move past it, your children may begin to feel responsible for your feelings or happiness. Allow God to bless you through His ministry of comfort. You'll then be better able to "freely give" to your children (Matthew 10:8)!

Special Thoughts for Blended Families

Adults in a blended family may also need to mourn the pain that comes prior to blending a family. It will be important for you to identify any unresolved losses related to divorce or death. Then together with your spouse, talk about your feelings, hurts, and losses. Grieve and receive comfort so that you will be free to respond adequately to your children. Your sensitivity to your own struggles will increase your sensitivity to your children.

You and your spouse may also find it necessary to spend some time grieving the loss of the "perfect family." You will then need to comfort one another.

As with any family, the blended family must face the positive and negative experiences that go along with relationships. Don't deny the challenges of blending two families, but focus on the opportunities you have together. By God's special grace and the Spirit's leadership, your spouse can actually come to comfort you over the pain and loss of previous relationships, whether the losses were due to death or divorce. The blessing of such comfort is a powerful testimony of God's miraculous grace.

Experiencing Biblical Truth

"Rejoice with those who rejoice;
Mourn with those who mourn." (Romans 12:15)

1. Set a time and place with your partner to share with each other your thoughts and feelings about your growing up years. Make sure you can allow an hour or more of uninterrupted time together.
2. Decide who will go first. That person should then share what was recorded earlier in this chapter in the "Facing Our Emotions" section. As much as possible, seek to allow any emotions to come to the surface.
3. Respond to any expressions of emotion with the corresponding emotions. Be joyful with your partner for anything which was good. Mourn with your partner over anything which your partner feels sadness about. Rejoice and mourn fully for one partner before the other partner begins sharing.
4. The second partner should then do the above, expressing both joy and sadness and receiving rejoicing and mourning as appropriate.
5. After both partners are finished, reflect on your experience of Romans 12:15. What feelings do you have about experiencing care like this, both joy and comfort? How did it feel to share both your gratefulness and sadness and then have someone rejoice and mourn with you? Write your response here:

_____

_____

_____

_____

[Ex: *I felt cared for when my partner listened to me and expressed her sadness for what I had experienced. Or, I felt loved when I saw tears in my spouse's eyes. He understood my hurt. I can sense he really cares! Or, It was important to me that my husband recognize and share with me the good things from my family.*]

6. What implications do you think the above has for you in your marriage and parenting relationships?

Homework for Our Homes

Experience the truth of Romans 12:15 with your children this week. Look for opportunities both to rejoice with them and mourn with them.

1. Pray, asking god to make you aware of any times of joy, being honored, or occasions of blessing your children may be experiencing.
2. When you are aware that something positive is being experienced, rejoice with them! Be happy with and for your kids, even though you may not feel very good at the time.

    Your words may sound like, "Wow, that's great! I'm very happy for you!" These expressions prevent your children from rejoicing alone!
3. Pray, asking God to make you keenly aware of any times of disappointment, discouragement, hurt, or sadness for your kids.
4. As you notice these painful feelings, listen attentively and then share words of comfort.

    Your words might sound like, "It makes me sad to hear about . . ." or "I feel sad for you. I know that must have hurt." Give your children the opportunity to receive the blessing of mourning and receiving God's comfort given through you!

Chapter 5

———— ■ ————

A HOME ENVIRONMENT
FOR INTIMACY

(EXPERIENCING THE TRUTH OF GOD'S GRACE)

A child's home environment has a tremendous impact on whether he flourishes or flounders. In our "parenting with intimacy" journey, we care deeply about whether home is a place of liberty or bondage.

What makes the difference? Is there a type of "home environment" which promotes liberty instead of bondage? If so, what is it?

Parenting with intimacy means doing everything we can to teach and model through our actions and instruct with our words the grace and truth of Jesus Christ, the One who was full of grace and truth (John 1:14). We sometimes call this "Great Commandment Parenting," where we are seeking to help our children grow up to "love the Lord" and "love their neighbor," (Matthew 22:37-39). Clearly, in order for this to occur, our children must experience both God's love and our love for them. This is why we stress taking the initiative to give to meet our children's needs!

Now at this point, we're raising a more subtle question, but one which is every bit as important:

What "atmosphere" should pervade our homes? What fundamental qualities should characterize our home environments? What's most important to consistently demonstrate in order to treat our children as God treats us?

We suggest one word: GRACE! A home environment which fosters intimacy with God and intimacy with each other will be an environment of grace, modeling to our children the One who was "full of grace," (John 1:14), who "gives us His fullness, grace upon grace," (John 1:16), "through whom grace was realized," (John 1:17).

But why is a "grace environment" at home so important?

The first reason is this: **our children will not experience a grace environment in the world.** Our homes are where God intends our children to first come to know and receive grace.

The "world system" which permeates our society is the system of **"doing things"** in order to **"be ok."** We work to keep jobs and work even harder to get raises. The system says **Performance = Worth.** The emphasis is on **what we do,** not on **who we are.** This "performance-based-worth" system is one we all live in and must learn to function in as a necessary part of growing up. We are "in the world," but we don't have to be "of this world!" (John 17:16).

In addition, children are rapidly developing their belief system about themselves and others, about God and family, and about the world and how it works. They are constantly assimilating messages received both verbally and nonverbally. As we would expect, many of the messages coming their way reflect this world system of Performance = Worth.

What's critically important to remember is this: Children strongly tend to believe all messages from Mom, Dad, and other important authority figures (older siblings, other family members, other important adults, and even the media!). Both true and false messages are cataloged as if they are true—whether they are or not.

What message are they receiving at home about performance and worth? Performance = Worth? Or something very different?

God says to us that our performance is important— *"Whatever you do, work at it with all your heart, as working for the Lord, not for men,"* (Colossians 3:23).

But working hard does not earn us a relationship with Him: *"He saved us, not on the basis of deeds which we have done in righteousness, but according to His mercy, by the washing of regeneration by the Holy Spirit"* (Titus 3:5). *"For it is by grace you have been saved, through faith—and this not from your-selves, it is the gift of God—not by works, so that no one can boast,"* (Ephesians 2:8-9). The only thing we've earned is death: *"The wages of sin is death,"* (Romans 3:23).

Nor does performance earn His love for us expressed in meeting our needs (Philippians 4:19). As we established in Chapter 1, all of us are born with needs, such as acceptance, approval, and comfort. An important question to ask is, what must we "do" in order to receive them? Must they be earned through *acceptable performance* or are they *freely given to us?*

Consider this question: **What did we do to earn...**

◆ **God's Love?**

"And walk in love, just as Christ also loved you, and gave Himself up for us, an offering and a sacrifice to God as a fra-grant aroma" (Ephesians 5:2).

◆ **God's Acceptance?**

"Accept one another, then, just as Christ accepted you." (Romans 15:7).

◆ **God's Kindness and Forgiveness?**

"Let all bitterness and wrath and anger and clamor and slander be put away from you, along with all malice. And be kind to one another, tender-hearted, forgiving each other, just as God in Christ also has forgiven you" (Ephesians 4:31-32).

◆ **God's Comfort?**

"Blessed be the God and Father of our Lord Jesus Christ, the Father of mercies and God of all comfort; who comforts us in all our affliction so that we may be able to comfort those who are in any affliction with the comfort with which we ourselves are comforted by God" (II Corinthians 1:4).

The answer is obvious—We did *nothing* to earn or deserve these things. Christ set the precedent. He established the pattern. He gave freely; we received. Therefore, as we have freely received, we are to freely give (Matthew 10:8).

Trying to live on the world's performance treadmill leads nowhere and hinders relationships in the process. The broad path of performance-based-acceptance is one that many families travel, but its end is destructive. The narrow path of unconditional giving is one that few families travel, but its end is greatly blessed.

Consider the following chart which contrasts the "world's system" with "God's system." It summarizes key elements and outcomes in a home filled with the liberty of grace. It also shows the contrast with relationships of this world—filled with conditions, performance pressure and fear.

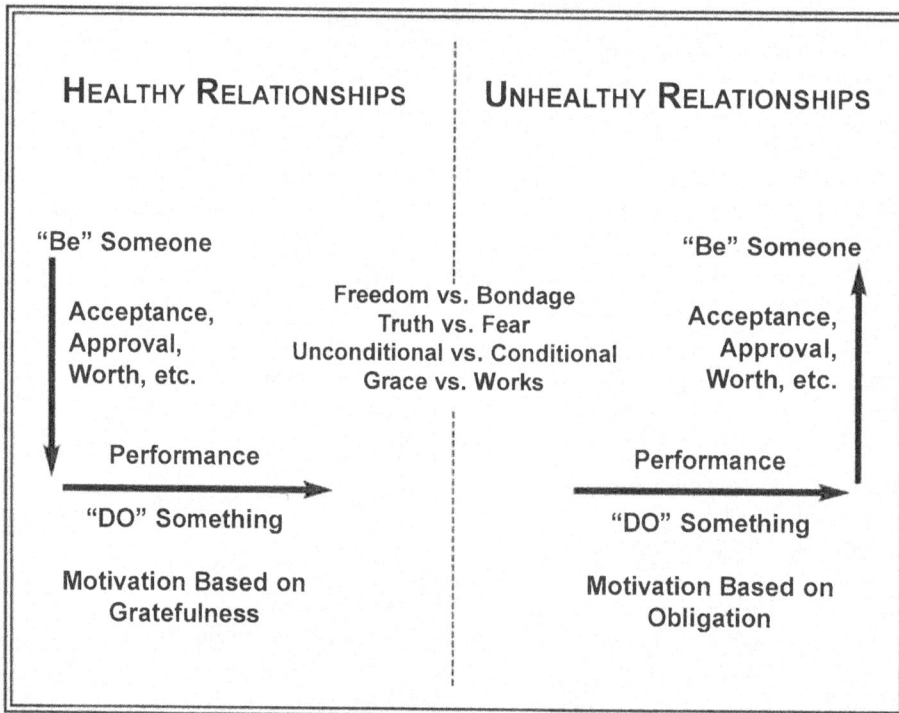

HEALTHY RELATIONSHIPS		UNHEALTHY RELATIONSHIPS
"Be" Someone		"Be" Someone
Acceptance, Approval, Worth, etc.	Freedom vs. Bondage Truth vs. Fear Unconditional vs. Conditional Grace vs. Works	Acceptance, Approval, Worth, etc.
Performance		Performance
"DO" Something		"DO" Something
Motivation Based on Gratefulness		Motivation Based on Obligation

"Be" then "Do." It's essential to keep the correct order. Intimate relationships are founded upon first *"being"* accepted, loved, and valued. Then a desire to *"do"* things consistent with this acceptance, love, and worth will tend to follow.

STOP AND CONSIDER

Stop and consider Jesus Christ's gifts to you. Christ freely gives you love, acceptance, forgiveness, and comfort. He loves you for who you are, not just what you do. Is your heart touched by these unconditional gifts? What feelings do you have toward the Savior?

Write your words to Jesus here:

_____

_____

_____

_____

_____

Obedience Motivated by Gratefulness: Inspired by the Experience of Grace

The other reason why a "grace environment" at home is so important: **it fosters the only internal motivation toward lasting obedience: Love for God prompted by gratefulness for what we have received from Him.** *"If you love me, you will obey my commandments,"* John 14:15.

Every parent longs for, yes, even prays for obedient children. It's appropriate to want to raise responsible children who are obedient to parents, appropriate authority figures and, of course, God. It's not sufficient, though, to simply observe a child's positive outward behaviors, pat ourselves on the back, and congratulate ourselves on a job well done. We must look beneath the surface of obedience to see what's *motivating* the good behaviors. It matters not just that children are doing good, but also *why* they are doing good.

Imagine we've employed a video surveillance camera to document the comings and goings of two young boys, Timothy and Daniel for a month. At the end of that month, we watch the film and see exactly the same thing. Both boys appear to be obedient, polite, dutiful young men. But we know nothing about what's going on beneath the surface—in their hearts—why they are obedient.

Let's suppose that Timothy's obedience is motivated by fear—fear that he might lose his parents' love if he doesn't perform according to their expectations, fear of failure, fear of negative consequences, or fear that his needs will go unmet if he doesn't do everything perfectly. Performing out of fear, duty, or obligation may look good for a time, but seldom sustains obedience over the long haul. Jesus said, "If you love Me, you'll obey My commandments," not if you fear Me or something else, you'll obey My commandments.

Doing things in order to gain the approval, acceptance, and love of others becomes a hollow accomplishment. What happens when Timothy goes to college and that fear of parental disapproval is no longer as pervasive? Behavior that looked good on the surface may turn to irresponsibility that will hinder him from reaching his God-given potential.

Suppose Daniel's obedience is motivated by gratefulness for having already received approval, acceptance, and love from his parents and from God. Knowing that his parents consider him a valuable "gift" from the Lord, he will tend likewise to be motivated to be a wise steward of his God-given talents and abilities.

"Wishful thinking!" you may respond. We agree that Daniel may also be motivated in part by the threat or fear of certain negative consequences of disobedience. The issue we are raising is whether it is possible for children (and us) to be *primarily motivated by a desire to please God, and parents and a "fear" of hurting and wronging God, parents, and others—all prompted by gratefulness and love for what we have received from God and parents.*

Let's not put too much emphasis on outward appearances. Let's keep in mind that the central issues are issues of the heart. Man looks at the outward appearance; God looks at the heart, (1 Samuel 16:7).

Let's also consider our perfect example, Jesus with His Father. In the Gospel accounts of Jesus' first day of public ministry we find Him going down to the Jordan River to submit Himself to John for baptism. First, He hears the testimony of John: *"Behold, the Lamb of God who takes away the sin of the world!"* Then comes confirmation of even greater significance. As He comes up out of the water, the heavens open, the Spirit of God descends upon Him like a dove, and a voice speaks: *"You are my Beloved Son in whom I am well pleased."* Let's stop right there. We miss the whole import of this passage if we think that was said for the crowd's benefit. To the contrary, this was the Heavenly Father affirming His Child. *"You are my Beloved Son in whom I am well pleased."* The beautiful part of this story is that God the Father affirmed Jesus before he had ever preached a sermon or performed a miracle. He blessed Him because of who He *was*, not because of what He'd *done*.

After Jesus was blessed by His Father, He spent forty days and forty nights in the wilderness. He was repeatedly tempted by the devil but did not succumb to temptation. Perhaps it was His Father's blessing that sustained Him! And could it be that part of what prompted, undergirded, and motivated the earthly ministry of Jesus was an overwhelming sense of gratefulness for that blessing? As He ministered during the ensuing three years of His life, He was intimately acquainted with sorrow and grief but surely had those words locked in His heart and ringing in His ears—*"You are my Beloved Son in whom I am well pleased."*

Apply the principles

This week, approach each of your children and for no apparent reason say something like, *"I was reminded again today how much I love you and how proud I am to have you as my son (or daughter)."* Then just hug your child and walk on. Leave your kid standing there in the awe and wonder of "What did I do to deserve that?" The only possible conclusion? Nothing! Share this scriptural blessing and other such expressions of unconditional grace and love, over time will tend to produce an empowering sense of gratefulness in your children.

Unconditionally loving your children "frees" them from performing in order to please people. Having truly partaken of grace, they are genuinely free to give to others. Having received that which they could not earn and did not deserve (i.e. grace), they are therefore free from fear of never having it and the fear of ever losing it.

Grace Takes the Initiative to Give

How might we as parents help our kids experience the awe and wonder of grace? **What does a "home environment for intimacy" characterized by grace really look like?**

Divine grace initiates our intimate relationship with God. It was Christ who humbled Himself, took on the form of a servant, and became obedient to the point of death (Phillipians 2:7-10). It was Christ who left His world and entered into ours. In a similar way, as parents, we need to take initiative to really know our children, enter into their world and meet needs as good stewards of God's divine grace.

We would like to offer several practical ways for you to take initiative in sharing God's grace with your children:

Initiate prayer.

Prayer is an important part of family closeness. Prayer can come with gratefulness at times of joy or with burdens at times of pain. You might try praying "over" your children. Slip into your child's room and quietly pray. Begin this at an early age and continue it even as your children work through the tough spots of adolescence. You might even want to let your secret "slip"—as your children hear about your prayers they'll sense your love and concern.

Pray for your children. Begin a prayer list of key issues for each child. You might pray for spiritual openness or your child's personal relationship with Christ. You could pray for character qualities you'd like to see developed in your child, freedom from specific struggles or even for their future ministry, career, and family.

Pray with your children. After bedtime reading and at meal times are good places to start, but be sure to keep these prayers personal—not just formalities. Take advantage of birthdays, holidays, special celebrations to share prayers of joy and gratitude. Encourage each child to pray as they feel comfortable

Initiate confessions.

Let's reiterate what we established in a previous chapter: All parents are imperfect human beings. Consequently, we all make mistakes, have weaknesses, and display inconsistencies. The crucial issue is, do we try to perpetuate the lie of infallibility, or do we vulnerably admit our human imperfections?

Healthy families deal with the inevitable reality that we hurt and wrong each other. One of the most powerful ways to deal with the hurts that occur within the family is through confession and forgiveness. How long has it been since your children heard you genuinely apologize for some wrong? If you are aware of ways you have hurt your spouse or your children, take the initiative to confess to God and then to your family members. Hearing, "I was wrong, will you forgive me?" sends a powerful message to a child. It communicates a sense of value as well as gives them permission to make mistakes and deal with them productively: "If Mom and Dad can admit mistakes, then I can admit my mistakes; and if Mom and Dad can be forgiven for their mistakes, so can I. What a relief!"

Apply the principles

Think back to the last time you gave a sincere apology to your child. What did your confession "sound like?"

A genuine confession does not include phrases such as ...

- "If I upset you..." (Minimizing your child's hurt)
- "I know I lost my temper, but if you hadn't disobeyed me, I wouldn't have ..." (Blaming your child for your wrong behavior)
- "I realize that I should have _____, but I had a terrible day." (Excusing your own wrong)

A genuine confession includes humble acknowledgment of specific wrong, without explanation or justification. (For example: "*Michael, I was wrong to raise my voice to you. It was wrong of me to lose my temper. Will you forgive me?*")

Ask God to bring to your mind one way that you have wronged your child that now needs confession. Consider the possibilities of broken promises, angry outbursts, disrespectful words, name calling, harsh punishment, etc. Write about what God brings to your mind here:

*I have wronged my child by:*_____
_____
_____
_____

Confess this to God now. Experience His promise to forgive and cleanse you: "*If we confess our sins, He is faithful and just to forgive us our sins and to cleanse us from all unrighteousness,*" (I John 1:9):

Dear God, I agree with you that I have wronged my child by . . .

[Express to God what you wrote in the above space.]

Thank you for your forgiveness and cleansing!

Now go to that child. Confess your wrongs and pray for your child that God would heal your child of the effects and the pain of your wrongdoing. Experience the blessing of James 5:16: *"Confess your sins to each other and pray for each other so that you may be healed."*

Initiate Giving
Appreciation and Approval

Since intimate relationships thrive upon accepting one another for who we are rather than what we do, it's important to communicate our approval of a person's character as well as appreciation for their behavior. The results are powerful. Expressing appreciation and approval affirms a person's divinely declared worth and encourages living in a manner "worthy of the calling" (Ephesians 4:1).

Familiarize yourself with the following list of character qualities and look for opportunities to affirm your children as they demonstrate these qualities. Try verbal affirmations, notes in their school lunches, or notes on the refrigerator door. If you're away from home, you might want to leave a message on the answering machine or send an affirming e-mail. Discovering and expressing appreciation for your children's character traits communicates a genuine desire to build them up. As they sense that desire on your part, they will feel a greater freedom to come to you with the hurts and disappointments they will inevitably experience.

Apply the principles

Here's a great method for verbalizing words of appreciation to your child.

♦ Identify 1-2 character qualities you see in your child.

♦ Get down on your child's eye level, make eye contact and maybe even put your hand on a shoulder or hold hands.

♦ Finish this sentence: "One of the special qualities I see in you is ..."
    * Name the quality.
    * Tell about a recent occasion when your child demonstrated that quality.
♦ Make this a habit, sharing words of appreciation at least once a week.

Even young children will know you're communicating loving words even if they don't fully understand the meaning of the words. The thirty seconds it takes to complete those sentences will cultivate a home environment saturated with grace!

30 Selected Character Qualities

1. ACCEPTANCE - deliberate and ready reception with a favorable response; to receive someone unconditionally and willingly (Rom. 15:7)

2. CAUTIOUSNESS -gaining adequate counsel before making decisions; recognizing temptations and fleeing them (Prov. 11:14)

3. COMPASSION - feeling the hurts of others and doing all that is possible to relieve them (I Pet. 3:8)

4. CONTENTMENT - enjoying present possessions rather than desiring new or additional ones; being happy regardless of circumstances (I Tim. 6:6)

5. CREATIVITY - finding godly solutions to difficult problems; discovering practical applications for spiritual principles (Rom. 12:12,21)

6. DECISIVENESS - finalizing difficult decisions on the basis of God's ways, word, and will (Jas. 4:15)

7. DEFERENCE - limiting my freedom to not offend those God has called me to serve (Rom. 14:13)

8. DEPENDABILITY - being true to your word even when it is difficult to carry out what promised to do (Matt. 5:37)

9. DILIGENCE - seeing every task as an assignment from the Lord and applying energy and concentration to accomplish it (Col. 3:23-24)

10. DISCERNMENT/SENSITIVITY knowing what to look for in evaluating people, problems and things; saying the right words at the right time (Eph. 4:29)

11. ENDURANCE/PERSEVERANCE - maintaining commitment to what is right during times of pressure (Rom. 5:3-4)

12. FAITH - developing an unshakable confidence in God's Word and visualizing God's will and acting upon it (Heb. 11:6)

13. FORGIVENESS - choosing to not hold an offense against another, remembering how much God has forgiven us (Eph. 4:32)

14. GENEROSITY - recognizing that all possessions belong to God; learning how to be a wise steward of time, money, and possessions; being a cheerful giver (II Cor. 8:9, 9:7)

15. GENTLENESS - responding to needs with kindness and love; knowing what is appropriate to meet the emotional needs of others (Eph. 4:2)

16. GRATEFULNESS - recognizing the benefits which God and others have provided; looking for appropriate ways to express genuine appreciation (Eph. 5:20)

17. HOSPITALITY - sharing what we have with those whom we don't know; "love of strangers" (I Pet. 4:9)

18. HUMILITY - recognizing our total inability to accomplish anything good apart from God's grace; recognizing our fundamental "neediness" (Eph. 4:2)

19. INITIATIVE - taking steps to seek after God with our whole heart; giving first rather than waiting for others to give (Luke 6:38)

20. LOYALTY - adopting as your own the wishes and goals of those you are serving (Col. 3:22)

21. MEEKNESS - yielding our rights and possessions to God; being willing to earn the right to be heard rather than demanding a hearing (I Pet. 5:6)

22. PATIENCE - accepting difficult situations as from God without giving Him or others a deadline to remove the problem (I Cor. 13:4)

23. PUNCTUALITY - showing esteem for other people and their time by not keeping them waiting (Phil. 2:3-4)

24. REVERENCE - demonstrating to God and others respect for the authority and character of God (Prov. 1:7)

25. SECURITY - entrusting our needs and expectations to Christ based upon His eternal Word (I Pet. 5:7; Phil. 4:6-7)

26. SELF-CONTROL - identifying and obeying the promptings of the Holy Spirit; bringing our thoughts, words, and actions under the control of the Holy Spirit (Eph. 5:18)

27. SINCERITY- having motives that are transparent; having a genuine concern to benefit the lives of others (Rom. 12:9)

28. TRUTHFULNESS - gaining approval of others without misrepresenting the facts; facing the consequences of a mistake; telling the whole truth (Eph. 4:25)

29. VIRTUE - demonstrating personal moral standards which cause others to desire a more godly life (I Tim. 4:12)

30. WISDOM - seeing life from God's perspective; learning how to apply principles of scripture in practical situations (Col. 1:9-10)

Why not set your sights on a new goal—establishing a heritage of grace with your children through initiating experiences of grace. Dream of your children saying, "My parents gave love to me ..."

◆ through the undivided attention they gave me.
◆ through their patient listening to my hurts and fears.
◆ through their empathy and openness as we shared feelings.
◆ through their valuing my thoughts and opinions.
◆ through their willingness to let me try some of my own decisions and plans.
◆ through the common interests and fun we shared.
◆ through their verbalized appreciation and love.
◆ through their openness to touch, hug and reassure me just with their presence.
◆ through their praying with me regularly about my concerns and needs
◆ through their involving me in church activities that I enjoyed

Scripture Reflection and Prayer
I John 4:4

"As you therefore have received Christ Jesus the Lord, so walk in Him, having been firmly rooted and now being built up in Him and established in your faith, just as you were instructed, and overflowing with gratitude."

"Greater is He who is in you, than he who is in the world."

The challenge is great—raising children who experience the security of being loved unconditionally and who thus "perform"—loving God and others fervently from the heart— motivated by gratefulness for His loving grace in the midst of a world that is increasingly hostile toward them.

But the promises of God's Word provide solace and encouragement. Take a moment and thank the Lord that He is stronger than any adversary and will guide and protect you as you seek to be a parent committed to providing a safe, loving home environment for your children.

Lord, thank you that I can count on you that . . .

_____

_____

_____

_____

_____

Special Thoughts For Single Parents

Loving children for who they are means communicating that love appropriately. Be careful of the traps that come with material possessions. Avoid the power struggle of competing with another parent or family in giving money or gifts. Avoid trying to buy your way into your child's life. Seize the moments available to give what money can't buy. Taking initiative to give to our children as outlined in this chapter is more important than financial status.

Prepare to answer the tough questions, if you haven't already. Show your commitment to acceptance by helping your child understand the divorce or death and cope with the results. Be sure your children know the loss was in no way their fault. Affirm them for the positive character qualities you observe in their lives. This will alleviate the tendency to feel that if they had just been more perfect, the loss would not have occurred.

Special Thoughts For Blended Families

A significant concern for many blended families involves what may be happening in the other home environment your children spend time in. The other home may manifest an environment of strict legalistic "rules and regulations are all that matter." Or it may be an environment characterized by "anything goes" or "if it feels good, do it."

If you find yourself concerned, consider the following: It may be difficult to accept, but typically, efforts to control other home environments bear little fruit and may even become worse through our efforts. Certainly discussions of your concerns with the other key people should occur. But just as important: Focus on having oneness between parents in your home. Realize that differences and inconsistencies are almost inevitable between two home environments. If properly dealt with, these challenges can enhance a child's maturity. Challenging situations can mold a child's personal value system and deepen his or her convictions. Try not to fight the battle of insisting on common behaviors and rules for two homes, but focus on giving abundantly to a child's relational needs.

Another sometimes difficult task that every stepparent must face is loving stepchildren. Love begins with acceptance. Therefore, you may not experience all of the tender emotions that are present with a "birth" child, but acceptance of stepchildren is still our responsibility. Avoid the tendency to focus solely on a stepchild's behavior by finding positive character traits about each stepchild. Then think of practical ways you can express your appreciation and reinforce these traits. By changing your focus, you may begin to see the child with more accepting eyes. And as they sense your acceptance of who they are, their behavior may even change.

Experiencing Biblical Truth

As we have said in this chapter, part of developing a "Grace Environment" within our homes involves cultivating the habit of appreciating others. Experience Ephesians 4:29 with your spouse or partner:

1. Look over the list of 30 Selected Character Qualities and circle two character qualities you see in your spouse or partner.
2. Turn to your partner. Make eye contact. Say the person's name as you begin the appreciation.
3. Share these words with your partner: "Wayne, one of the character qualities I see in you is ....."
   * Name the quality.

* Read the definition aloud.

* Tell about a recent occasion when your partner demonstrated that quality.

For example: *Wayne, one of the character qualities I see in you is diligence. Diligence means that you see every task as an assignment from the Lord and apply energy and concentration to accomplish it. You demonstrated diligence in shopping for our car. You spent several weeks looking for the best price and best value. Our nice car reflects your character quality of diligence!*

For example: *Debbie, one of the character qualities I see in you is sensitivity. Sensitivity means knowing what to look for in evaluating people, problems and things. Saying the right words at the right time. You have been very sensitive during our sharing today. You've known what to say as I've shared my parenting struggles with you. You've definitely said the right words at the right time.*

4. After the above has been completed, receive your partner's appreciation by saying, "Thank you!"
5. Switch roles. Take turns appreciating each other's character qualities until you've affirmed the two or more you've selected.
6. How did you feel after giving and receiving appreciation? (Connected, affirmed, blessed, loved, valued, encouraged, etc.)

_____

_____

_____

_____

_____

_____

_____

Homework for Your Homes

1. Select two qualities you see in each of your children (ages 3 and older).

Name of Child	Character Quality	Character Quality
_____	_____	_____
_____	_____	_____
_____	_____	_____
_____	_____	_____

2. Plan a time to appreciate each child in the next few days. You may or may not read the definition of the character quality, but each child will benefit from your affirming words and loving initiative. Your appreciation might sound like: *David, I noticed today how kind and compassionate you are. I heard you tell Andrew that you were sorry his bike got stolen. I'll bet your words made him feel better.*

Chapter 6

———— ■ ————

HELPING OUR CHILDREN
RESOLVE PAINFUL EMOTIONS
(DEALING WITH HURT, ANGER, GUILT AND FEAR)

Even the most adventurous among us would have to agree that when facing uncharted territory, our comfort level increases dramatically when the expertise of a tour guide is available. A "guided tour" implies that the one in a position of leadership has been down this road before and knows the ins and outs, the "must sees" and "must dos" as well as the "danger zones." Imagine how disconcerting it would be if you were faithfully following your trusted guide down a narrow trail and innocently asked, "Where does this road lead?" only to hear, "Don't know. Never been down this particular road before. Guess we'll find out together."

The Warren family recently drove to San Antonio for a much-needed mini-vacation. On their way, they stopped at the Inner Space Caverns in Georgetown, Texas. They arrived just in time to join a large group of energetic, eager, wide-eyed children from a local school. Rather than wait several hours to take a more "age-appropriate" tour, they decided to tag along with these would-be-explorers and their adult companions.

The tour guide had obviously done his homework. His knowledge of the history of the caverns and the intricacies and distinguishing characteristics of each type of formation was impressive. The children were, of course, bubbling with curiosity. He patiently and respectfully answered each question, no matter how small or how silly. At one point, he leaned over to Paul and whispered, "Too bad you had to come today. If you were on another tour I'd be able to give you a lot more detailed information." Paul and Matthew would probably have appreciated that since they're the scientific-types in the Warren house-hold! Vicky was actually quite satisfied with the level of explanation. She was impressed with the fact that their guide was able to adapt his instruction to whatever level was needed. That's not an easy task!

As our children travel their yet-uncharted road toward maturity, they are looking to us to be effective, knowledgeable, helpful "tour guides." It may not be appropriate for us to tell them "everything" we know—that might scare them! Instead, we should strive to identify and address their "need of the moment." Ephesians offers some sound direction in this

---

We are all created with an íemotional capacityíóa part of our brain which actually stores and processes emotions.

---

regard: *"Let no unwholesome word proceed from your mouth, but only such a word as is good for edification according to the need of the moment, that it may give grace to those who hear,"* (Ephesians 4:29, NASB). This truth is particularly important in helping children learn to deal with painful emotions.

Parenting with intimacy requires knowing our children's emotions and then lovingly guiding and directing them in how to scripturally resolve them. In this chapter, we'd like to offer you our "guided tour" of emotions—specifically, a tour of painful emotions. We'd like to look at five difficult emotions every child will face. We'll look at each painful feeling and give you practical, Scriptural principles for how to respond to your children when they are experiencing them. As we experience the biblical principles of this chapter, both we and our children can learn to identify, respond to, and resolve painful emotions.

As we begin the tour, let's cover some important general information. First, we are all created with an "emotional capacity"—a part of our brain which actually stores and processes emotions. In a sense this part of our brains acts as an "emotional cup," the place where we all "hold" both positive and painful emotions.

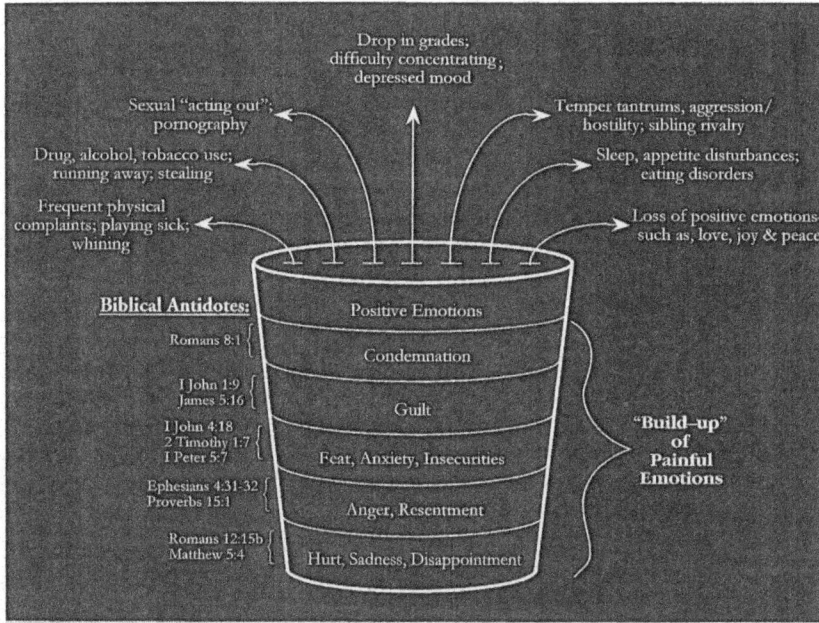

Drop in grades; difficulty concentrating; depressed mood

Sexual "acting out"; pornography

Drug, alcohol, tobacco use; running away; stealing

Frequent physical complaints; playing sick; whining

Temper tantrums, aggression/ hostility; sibling rivalry

Sleep, appetite disturbances; eating disorders

Loss of positive emotions— such as, love, joy & peace

Biblical Antidotes:

Romans 8:1

I John 1:9
James 5:16

I John 4:18
2 Timothy 1:7
I Peter 5:7

Ephesians 4:31-32
Proverbs 15:1

Romans 12:15b
Matthew 5:4

Positive Emotions

Condemnation

Guilt

Fear, Anxiety, Insecurities

Anger, Resentment

Hurt, Sadness, Disappointment

"Build-up" of Painful Emotions

Picture a young boy named Tommy. Like all of us, Tommy has this capacity within to "hold emotions"—his "cup" fills up with emotion as Tommy experiences life's events. When Tommy wins his baseball game, he feels excited and happy and these feelings go into his emotional cup. When a classmate makes fun of Tommy, feelings of hurt and anger go into his emotional cup.

But just like a literal cup, Tommy's emotional cup can only hold so much emotion. When his cup is full, it begins to overflow. If Tommy's cup has been filled with positive emotions such as joy, peace, love and contentment, he will tend to "overflow" with positive and appropriate behavior. We might notice fewer physical complaints, greater ability to concentrate, fewer outbursts of anger, and more self control.

But if Tommy's cup has been filling up with painful emotions such as hurt, anger, and fear we might see painful and unhealthy symptoms overflow. We might see Tommy "overflow" with things like stomach aches and temper tantrums. We might see an increase in whining, more frequent nightmares, or more difficulty concentrating on his studies.

Study the diagram on the previous page (141), considering how it might describe your children:

Tommy's parents might typically tend to focus mostly on Tommy's symptoms—his behavior. Obviously they can see his behavior and may be very bothered by it! What else could they do?

Remember the "Zacchaeus Principle" from Chapter 2? We asserted that parenting with intimacy requires identifying "the need beneath the deed" and seeking to meet it. Now we're exploring a very important related concept—the emotions beneath the deeds! As loving parental "tour-guides" to our children, we'll want to look beneath the symptoms to help them first identify the feelings underneath. Then, since God has given us Scriptural "antidotes"—ways of resolving each of the painful emotions, we can then teach our children how to "empty" the painful feelings according to the scriptural wisdom God has provided. Then they (and we) can experience more positive feelings and a decrease of the unproductive symptoms!

The Importance of Identifying Emotions

We will typically find it difficult to properly respond to or resolve emotions until we are able to identify them. Once an emotion can be called by its name it becomes less formidable and is no longer part of that great sea of unknowns facing a growing child. Kids are born feeling emotions, but they are not born with the ability to name them. Part of our job is to help our children develop a "feeling vocabulary."

So how about our own "feeling vocabulary?" How well do we identify our own emotions? Many of us can name only a few, such as: "bad" or "mad" or "fine."

But life is full of emotions! And the Bible portrays them fully as they are experienced by men, women, and children. Even

Jesus is portrayed with the full range of painful emotions: sadness ("*He was . . . a man of sorrows,*" Isaiah 53:3); anger: (*"He looked around at them in anger,"* (Mark 3:5); possibly even fear as He faced the crucifixion: *("and He began to be deeply distressed and troubled . . .",* Mark 14:33). The Holy Spirit and God the Father can be grieved and saddened (Genesis 6:6, Ephesians 4:30).

In order to better resolve them (and to be able to help our children do the same), we need to be able to begin by naming those feelings.

This is especially important because the "scriptural antidotes" are not the same—each emotion has its own specific antidote! For example, we're specifically directed to forgive (let go) of anger. Is that what we are to do with fear? (Check I John 4:18-19 to find out!) Thus we need to first learn how to identify the emotion so that we will apply the appropriate divine remedy!

What Are You Feeling?

Stop and consider the following list of 30 difficult/painful emotions:

Disappointed	Nervous	Rejected
Mad	Convicted	Resentful
Frustrated	Sorrowful	Discouraged
Scared	Lonely	Hopeless
Ashamed	*Worried*	Bitter
Frightened	Insecure	Regretful
Embarrassed	Disgusted	Confused
Remorseful	Jealous	Depressed
Sad	Worthless	Afraid
Anxious	Apologetic	Enraged

1. Hurt: _____ _____ _____

_____ _____ _____

2. Anger: _____ _____ _____

_____ _____ _____

3. Fear: _____ _____ _____

_____ _____ _____

4. Guilt: _____ _____ _____

_____ _____ _____

5. Condemnation: _____ _____ _____

_____ _____ _____

Quite a list isn't it? Is it possible these feelings are simply different forms of five basic emotions: hurt, anger, fear, guilt, and condemnation? How might you categorize the emotions in this list?

Beside each of the five emotions below, list the feelings from the above list which you sense could be "grouped" with that emotion. See if this grouping might simplify your understanding of and ability to identify your own feelings.

We are not trying to assert "hard and fast" categories, but we are seeking to give us some "handles" to reduce the complexity of the emotional dimension of life.

As we work to strengthen our own understanding of and ability to identify emotions, we'll be better equipped to appropriately deal with our own. We'll also tend to be more sensitive to the feelings of those around us.

Identifying "Painfully Tender" Emotions

It's important for kids to be able to distinguish different types of emotions.

Knock, Knock...Who's There?

"It's Hurt."

Before exploring this painful emotion, it's important to make a distinction between childhood depression and the specific emotion of sadness. Childhood depression is usually a combination of three painful emotions: sadness, anger, and anxiety. It lasts a longer period of time and can be more debilitating. Sadness by itself is a normal and unavoidable part of growing up, whereas depression is a more serious problem which may need medical attention.

No one is exempt from sadness. As we've pointed out, even Jesus experienced deep sadness. We often joke about John 11:35 being the verse of choice when it comes to Scripture memorization because it's the shortest verse in the entire Bible— *"Jesus wept."* It may be short, but it's actually quite profound and revealing. Jesus felt great sadness at the death of his friend, Lazarus, particularly as He saw the sadness of Mary. He felt this deep pain even though He knew that He was going to remove the source of the pain by raising Lazarus from the dead!

Sadness will inevitably be experienced by every child. It is part and parcel of growing up because the inevitable hurts, shuns, and cruelties of life press in on children just as surely as they do adults. Learning to deal with sadness and grief is an essential part of growing up, and yet children are seldom taught what to do with their sadness. Adults tend to be uncomfortable with their own sadness, not to mention that of their children. Consequently, a sense of aloneness is often added to the child's sadness.

Children's common internal questions hint at the loneliness of sadness:

> *"Does anybody know that I feel sad?"*
> *"Does anyone else feel sad?"*
> *"Will I feel sad forever?"*

These questions need to be answered, but not with correction, advice, facts, or pep talks. In other words, don't just try to make the sadness go away. Comments of correction or advice ("If you would have just..." or "If you hadn't...") don't remove a child's aloneness. Relating facts ("Everyone feels that way sometimes" or "It's not the end of the world") doesn't help a hurting child. Nor does giving pep talks ("It'll be better next time" or "Let's focus on the positive").

What is the Scriptural antidote
for hurt, pain and sadness?

Romans 12:15b tells us to "mourn with those who mourn." Responding to a child's sadness requires our compassionate emotional response of comfort. Matthew 5:4 was written for children as well as adults. *"Blessed are those who mourn for they shall be comforted..."* As a child experiences comfort at the point of their sadness, blessing comes as aloneness subsides. This removal of "aloneness" may be one of the most significant ingredients in parenting with intimacy.

Helping children experience our comfort in their sadness involves several steps. Each is vitally important and must be followed in an orderly sequence.

First, give children permission to be sad. Children shouldn't have to be "strong" so adults can lean on them for strength. Children shouldn't have to cover up their sadness so as to make life more convenient and hassle-free for adults. They must be allowed to cry and to talk about their sadness.

Second, let them know you feel sad for them because you love and care for them. Don't assume they already know you care. They need to hear and experience your care. They need comfort, and we give comfort through our presence as well as verbally: *"I feel sad for you. I feel sad to see you hurting. I want you to know I love you and am here for you."* These are words that build up and minister grace. (Ephesians 4:29)

Third, only after liberally offering your comfort, vulnerably share your own past experiences of sadness. Share times when you've felt sad. Be sensitive so as not to make it sound as though you're dismissing their sadness as unimportant. The goal is not to communicate, *"You think you've got it bad. That's nothing. Why, when I was your age, I had something happen that was really sad."* The goal of self-disclosure is to let them see you as a real person with real emotions who can empathize with how they're feeling. (For example: *"I remember feeling sad when my best friend moved away. I felt sad because I was really going to miss her. We were special friends."*)

Fourth, offer realistic hope. Acknowledge that the sadness is painful now but that better times will come. An important measure of this hope comes from your self-disclosure of your own past experiences of sadness. This gives reassurance to a children that even though they are sad, they can still experience the blessing of comfort and move on with life.

But note: it will be important to separate this part of the conversation from your caring self-disclosure so that it doesn't come across as discounting their sadness or sounding like a lecture. For example: After a day or two has passed, say, "*How would you like to write your friend a letter and tell her our plans for the summer? Even though she's moved, we still can invite her to visit us this summer."*)

It's imperative to give these aspects of comfort in the above order. Don't start by telling them why they should be hopeful. First, enter their world and minister to their aloneness through giving them permission to be sad, then comforting them, then sharing your own past experiences.

Apply the principles

What might comforting your child look like? Think about a recent time when one of your children felt sad. Your child might have been sad over: not being invited to a party, conflict with a friend, a broken promise, etc. Remembering the characteristics of comfort and the admonition of Romans 12:15, write out your responses here:

*My son/daughter recently felt sad when*_____

_____

_____

*I could give permission to be sad by saying*_____

_____

_____

(For example: *"I know you're feeling sad about missing the birthday party. It really hurts to feel left out."*)

*I could let my son or daughter know what I'm feeling for him/her by saying*_____

_____

_____

(For example: "*I am so sorry this has happened. I feel so sad for you when I know your feelings have been hurt.*")

I could share a little about myself by saying

_____

_____

(For example: "*I feel sad for you because I remember what it was like to really want to go to a party but not be invited.*")

*After a few days have passed, I could offer realistic hope by saying*_____

_____

_____

(For example: "*Thank you for sharing your sad feelings with me. I know you feel really down now, so let's ask God to bring some other friends for you to have fun with. He loves you and wants what's best for you. I know He'll provide.*")

"It's Anger"

Suppose anger answers the door—this time not masking some other emotion. Is it OK to be angry? Is it OK for *your* child to be angry? We've probably all said it or had it said to us as a child, "Don't you be angry with me young man (young woman)! You wipe that angry look off your face!"

There's a saying that goes like this: *All emotions are acceptable; but some behaviors are not.* Anger has gotten a pretty bad rap because it's often followed or manifested by unacceptable behaviors. Ephesians 4:26-27 acknowledges that we will be angry at times but it also addresses the appropriate expression of our anger. *"Be angry, and yet do not sin; do not let the sun go down on your anger, and do not give the devil an opportunity."*

How can we help our children "be angry and yet not sin?"

At this juncture, let's look at something we affectionately refer to as "The Teapot Principle." Imagine, if you will, Tim Teapot sitting on the burner. He's full of water, and as the fire is turned up he soon reaches the boiling point. As the water begins to churn, what happens? Eventually, Tim will begin to spout and make that shrill, annoying noise that teapots make. When this happens, what are our choices?

We could stand in front of Tim Teapot and say, "I just love to hear you spout, Timmy. It's so good to hear you actualize yourself. Go ahead, boil and spit. Just spout away. Get it all out! You'll feel better." But what's going to happen? Timmy's going to burn out; he'll become a charred, burned-out teapot!

Or we could take this approach: "Kids are to be seen and not heard. Anybody knows that what you need to do is go to the local hardware store, buy the biggest cork you can find, and stuff it in Tim's spout. That'll teach him to spout off in front of us! He'll think twice before he does that again!" We could accomplish this by expressing even stronger anger at Timmy, so that Timmy becomes afraid of our anger!

If we encourage Tim to simply stuff his anger, what will happen to him? He might explode as the pressure builds up. Or, he may become seriously depressed. Or, (this is actually a combination of the first two) he'll become bitter. Bitterness is simply unresolved anger which has been repeatedly stuffed. Hebrews 12:15 tells us not to let a root of bitterness grow up among us or it defile us. What does *defile* mean? Ruin, spoil, and render ineffective.

Teaching our children how to deal with their anger appropriately is every bit as important, probably more so, than teaching them to do school work, how to brush their teeth, how to ride a bike, how to manage their allowance, or how to cross a busy street.

If we don't let them "boil over" and we don't try to "cork" their anger, what specifically could we help them learn about how to deal with their anger?

1. *Help them identify the anger.* A young child does not have the language skills to sit down and tell you, "You know, Dad (Mom), I'm really angry. I noticed that my adrenaline is rising, and I feel this anger welling up inside me. I'd like to talk through the causes and sources of my anger with you and see if we can't come to some sort of healthy resolution because I know that otherwise I will suffer painful emotional consequences." Remember, if we can't name it, we will have difficulty controlling it. So the first step is to help your child identify the anger:

    "Boy, you look angry! I can tell you're really mad!"

2. *Give them permission to be angry.* You're not giving them permission to be disrespectful or destructive, but you're giving them permission to feel what they're feeling. You might have to remind them that it is OK to feel angry, but it is not OK to act disrespectfully or destructively out of the anger.

3. *Help them develop self-control (Galatians 5:22) through choosing to "cool off."* It may be necessary at first for parents to remove a child from the "fire." Call this time-out or a cool-

---

Teaching our children how to deal with their anger appropriately is every bit as important, probably more so, than teaching them to do school work.

---

ing off period. This may sound something like: *Tim, I sense that you may need a few moments to yourself to get control of your feelings. Let's take a break and then get back together in 15 minutes.* After a while, children may learn to initiate the "cooling off" rather than losing their temper. Note: both parents and children may occasionally need a few moments of solitude in order to gain control of the anger.

4. *Respond to your child with a "gentle answer" which "turns away wrath," (Proverbs 15:1).* Talk about what's prompting the anger. In a calm voice, rephrase your child's concerns. Reflect the content of what they say as well as the feelings associated. (For example: *"I can tell that you're angry with Brad. It sounds like you're upset because he's not respecting your privacy."*)

5. *Help your children learn to look "underneath" the anger for hurt or sadness which then needs comfort.* For example: *"I'm wondering if you're also upset about something Brad said. It sounds like you might be feeling hurt because he made fun of you."*

6. *Help your children identify intimacy needs which may be going unmet* and teach them how to express these needs in a loving way:

   Child: *"Dad, I'm really frustrated with my homework. I can't do anything right!"*

   Dad: *"Sounds like you may need some **support** with all that work. I'd be glad to give you some help with it."*

   Child: *"Mom, my bedtime is way too early. Why can't I stay up as late as Billy?"*

   Mom: *"I want you to know that it matters to me how you feel about this. I'm not promising that I'll change it, but I know that you need me to **respect** you by considering a change. I will pray about it and let you know. Is there anything else that I should be thinking about as I pray about it?*

   Parents can encourage this learning process even from the earliest ages:

   "Sammy, when you get fussy like you are now, I wonder if you're needing a hug? Come let me hold you and tell you a story." (Affection, Attention)

   "Aaron, your anger makes me wonder if something happened today at school that we need to visit about? I'd sure like to." (Comfort, Security)

   These "gentle answers" from parents help turn away wrath and get to the real needs of our children.

7. *Teach your children how to ask for God's help in dealing with anger.* Sound strange? Maybe. But doesn't God tell us

to pray about everything? "Everything" certainly includes our anger.

"Dear God, thank you for this dinner. Thank you for our warm house. Thank you for helping me with my history test. And, God, could you help me learn self-control so I can express my anger in the right way?"

Music to God's (and parents') ears!

8. *Incorporate into all the above principles encouragement to forgive.* Ephesians 4:31 urges us, *"Get rid of all bitterness, rage and anger, brawling and slander, along with every form of malice."* How are we to do this? The next verse gives the answer: *"Be kind and compassionate to each other,* forgiving each other, *just as in Christ God forgave you."*

Forgiveness means letting go of our anger—choosing to no longer hold on to it. It means no longer holding a grudge against someone—we take another "off our hook."

As we cultivate in our children gratefulness for the forgiveness they have received from God—that it is unconditional, total, and always available to be experienced through confession (I John 1:9), this gratefulness provides the basis for "forgiving as we have been forgiven."

How might we invite and encourage our children to forgive as a very important part of their experience of the above principles? What might it sound like?

"Johnny, I know Billy really hurt you, and you've gotten real mad at him as a result. It makes perfect sense that you would get so angry, given how he treated you. You were needing respect and he didn't respect you. I feel very sad for you about it because I love you so much . . . [Take as long as needed to comfort the child. Then . . .]

"God tells us in His word that we are to forgive others, just like He has forgiven us. Are you ready to forgive Billy for what he did to you? [Spend as much time as needed explaining what it means to forgive and how to experience it. Especially make sure that your child has genuinely experienced the joy and relief of God's forgiveness and thus a gratefulness for His forgiveness. You might even guide the child in a prayer expressing their forgiveness: *"Dear God, I know that you have forgiven me*

for all the wrong things I've done. You've let go of your anger against me, and you've taken me off your hook. Thank you that this is true. So right now in Jesus' name, just like you chose to forgive me, I choose to forgive Billy for being so mean to me today. I let go of my anger and take him off my hook. In Jesus name, Amen."

Apply the principles

Recall a recent time one of your children expressed anger. What was the issue? What were the circumstances? Write a few words that describe the situation here:

_____

_____

_____

In this same situation, how might you have helped identify the emotion and given permission to feel the anger? That might sound like:

_____

_____

_____

(For example: *"Boy, you're really mad. It looks like you're about to explode"* or *"I can see you're very angry. It's OK to feel angry, but let's be careful what we do with it!"*)

How might you help your child deal with anger without stuffing it or letting him rage? One or more of these tools may be necessary:

I could suggest a cooling-off period by saying,

_____

_____

_____

_____

I could suggest appropriate ways of expressing feelings by saying,

_____

_____

_____

(For example: "*It's OK to talk with me about feeling mad.*" Or, "*Why don't you shoot baskets until you're ready to talk calmly.*")

I can limit inappropriate ways of expressing anger by saying,

_____

_____

(For example: "*Feeling angry is OK, hitting your sister is not.*" Or, "*I can see that you're angry. I want to hear about your feelings, but kicking the walls is not appropriate. That needs to stop.*")

I can get to and comfort the hurt beneath the anger by saying,

_____

_____

_____

(For example: "*I see your anger, but I'm wondering if you're also feeling hurt . . . I can tell you're angry. Tell me about your hurt too— I'd like to hear about it.*")

Don't forget about the other principles of dealing with anger, especially encouraging your children to forgive!

"It's Fear"

All kids have fears (as do all adults, for that matter!). In fact, depending on the age of the child, those fears are pretty predictable...fear of the dark, fear of monsters under the bed, fear of animals, etc. It's important for us to help our children deal with fear, because when allowed to go unchecked, fear is probably the most destructive of all emotions. Most kids who manifest what we typically call "acting-out behaviors" are actually very scared. It's never "cool" to admit to being scared, so some kids would rather be perceived as hostile or disinterested to cover up their fears.

Scripture gives us the key to overcoming fear: "*There is no fear in love; but perfect love casts out fear*" (I John 4:18).

So, how can we help our children experience God's perfect love in order to "cast out" their fears?

Saying things like, *"That's the most ridiculous thing I ever heard of. You're too old to be afraid of that. Don't be a baby"* is unproductive. It will slam the communication door shut and hurt children. It might even make them more fearful and alone.

Neither can we *make* their fears go away. We can express God's love for them through acknowledging their fear and comforting them, helping them look at truth relevant to their fears, and reassuring them of our presence.

1. *Acknowledge and comfort their fears.* "I know it's really hard to be afraid. It doesn't feel good. I'm sad for you that you're so scared."
2. *Offer truthful reassurance.* "It looks to me like you might be feeling scared. Let's look at the situation. Let's explore the truth about the circumstances together."
3. *Give reassurance of your presence.* "I'm going to go through this with you. You can count on me to be here for you."

Consider this example. Most children have at least one friend whose parents have divorced. Consequently, when children hear parents arguing, it produces fears that perhaps this could happen to their families as well.

How might parents put these three principles for helping children deal with fears into practice? Fears of divorce might be properly addressed by saying something like: *"I know it might scare you when Dad and I disagree. I feel sad for you that you've been scared, because I love you! In case you're ever worried that we might get a divorce, I want you to know that we're committed to staying together. Even though we don't always agree about everything and sometimes get upset with each other, we love each other very much and are committed to healing our hurts and always being there for you."*

Another example: If a child is afraid of thunderstorms, acknowledging and comforting their fear, offering truthful reassurance and a commitment to "be there" might sound like, *"I*

Most children have at least one friend whose parents have divorced. Consequently, when children hear parents arguing, it produces fears that perhaps this could happen to their families as well.

---

know you're afraid of the storm. I'm saddened that you are. It sounds really mean, doesn't it? Kind of like somebody up in the sky is really mad. But that's just the noise the storm makes. Nobody's mad, and the weatherman said the storm should only last about another hour. Your mom and I are here with you, and we're not going to let anything bad happen to you. Would you like to read one of your favorite stories to take your mind off the storm?" (For younger children, if there is a persistent source of fear, you might try to find a story about the subject to read whenever the fear surfaces.)

Jesus' reassurance to us:
He'll always be with us!

One of the most precious promises in all of Scripture is, *"Lo, I am with you always"* (Matthew 28:20). As Christ's earthly ambassador to our children, we have an opportunity to give that same support to them by assuring them that we will walk through the scary situation with them. Let them know through words and actions that we will be with them. When they're little children, that means that in a literal, physical sense we'll be with them. As they get older, this takes on a more emotional or spiritual form. We can express that we'll pray for them and that we are available to help them work it out, or just listen.

Notice, we said "with" them. This is entirely different than saying, *"Oh, you poor baby. This is too scary for you. Let me handle this for you."* Or the other extreme, *"Yep, it's pretty scary all right. Hope you get through it. See you on the other side."* Instead, be with them in their fear—*"I can understand you're scared. I'm going to walk through this with you, and I know together we can face it."*

As we walk hand-in-hand with them (for the younger child perhaps literally and as they grow older, symbolically), they will draw strength from our love and support, just as we do from Christ's love.

Apply the principles

How might you help your child experience the truth of I John 4:18 in order that your child might "empty" fear from their "emotional cups?"

Helping my child experience genuine *love* might look like . . . (Use the following prompts to help you define it!)

1. *My son/daughter is currently struggling with these fears:* (Ex: storms, afraid of the dark, dogs, rejection, failure, etc.)

_____

_____

2. *I will help my child identify his fear by saying:*

_____

_____

_____

(For example: I'm wondering if you don't want to go to Kevin's house because you're afraid of his big dog. There's nothing wrong with being afraid. Sometimes I get scared too.)

3. *I will comfort my fearful child by saying:*

_____

_____

_____

(For example: I feel sad when I think about you feeling afraid.)

4. *Offer truthful reassurance* — I will reassure my child by saying:

_____

_____

(For example: Brittany, I will ask Kevin's mom to make sure that the dog is in the back yard while we're at their house. I know the dog is bigger than you, but he's a friendly dog. He won't hurt you. He hasn't hurt Kevin, and Kevin is just your size.)

5. *Reassuring your child of your presence* — I will help cast out my child's fear by reassuring him of my presence. This will sound like:

_____

_____

(For example: Brittany, I will be with you the whole time at Kevin's house. We'll be together having fun—And remember, I love you.)

It's imperative that we also address the issue of parents making decisions based on fear. This is perhaps the most destructive force warring against healthy parenting today. Fear can immobilize parents and render them ineffective. 2 Timothy 1:7 is a great verse for parents. It reminds us that the fear is not from God and it reassures us of what God wants to give us instead of fear: *"For God has not given us a spirit of timidity [fear], but of power and love and discipline [sound judgment]."* 2 Timothy 1:7.

Power — Ask God to remind you of the authority He's given to us as parents. Then ask Him to equip you with His presence and reassure you of His work on your behalf.

Love — Ask God to reveal His loving concern for you. Spend time in prayer and in His Word. Ask God to reveal His love to you directly and through other people.

Sound judgment — Ask God for wisdom and prayerfully approach Him and His Word. Respond to what He shows you and follow His lead, rather than being ruled by what you are afraid of.

"It's Guilt."

In the field of mental health, guilt has gotten a bad name. The early years of psychiatry taught that guilt was the worst thing ever foisted upon mankind by religion—an idea propagated and nurtured by, among others, Sigmund Freud. Of course, some at the other end of the spectrum convey an equally inappropriate perspective of guilt: "It's the only way you can motivate people to do anything!"

But what exactly is guilt? How is it different from the emotion of condemnation which can feel so similar?

Genuine guilt ultimately comes from the Spirit's conviction of wrong-doing according to God's standards (John 16:8). The focus is our behavior—what we've done—not who we are.

Genuine guilt always offers the opportunity for restitution and restoration of the relationship through confession and forgiveness. I John 1:9 promises *"If we confess our sins, He is faithful and just to forgive us our sins and to cleanse us from all unrighteousness."*

Thus, a significant way God uses the emotion of genuine guilt is to let us know that we've done something wrong so that we can then do what we need to do to restore the relationship through confession—whether between us and God or between parents and children.

"It's Condemnation"

In contrast with guilt, condemnation always aims at who we are—our person. It's feeling bad, hopeless, discouraged about ourselves rather than about what we've done. Guilt says, *"I did a bad awful, rotten, no-good thing."* Condemnation says, *"I am a bad, awful, rotten, no-good person."* And since I'm such a horrible person, then it's fruitless to attempt to confess wrongs, seek forgiveness, and make restitution, because there isn't anything I can do to make up for what I did, and no one would ever want to forgive me anyway! So why bother?

One of the beautiful things about appropriate discipline is it helps protect kids from vulnerability to condemnation. They learn that if they do something wrong, there are consequences, but with their parents' guidance they can face those consequences and move on. They discover that their parents never stop loving them because they loved them before, during, and after the wrong. This kind of discipline always occurs in the context of loving intimate relationships based on unconditional acceptance (what this workbook is mostly about!).

Adults must define and implement a system of discipline where everyone takes "ownership" of their inappropriate behavior and accepts consequences for that behavior. It's this atmosphere of ownership of responsibility that encourages a child to "own" the mistakes that are his and forgive and "let go of" the mistakes of others. The habit of confession and seeking forgiveness—where even adults are able to say, "I was wrong when . . ." helps children learn that conflicts and problems are not always their fault. Appropriate discipline and sharing confessions thus helps children avoid a build-up of condemnation in their "emotional cups."

(Note: Appropriate discipline is such a vital tool that we'll devote the entire next chapter to it!)

STOP AND CONSIDER

In your home, can family members who are genuinely guilty of wrongs receive both appropriate consequences and genuine forgiveness, and make restitution when necessary? Or, do family members experience condemnation for mistakes or wrongs? Which of these descriptions best represent the atmosphere of your home?

An atmosphere of *condemnation* might look or sound like:

◆ *"I sure wish I had a little girl who would give me hug."*
◆ *"If you keep doing that, God's gonna get you!"*
◆ *"If I were you, I wouldn't act like that in church. I wouldn't want God and everybody else mad at me."*
◆ *"It's all your fault! . . . You don't ever do anything right! . . . You'll never amount to anything! . . . I wish you had never been born!"*
◆ *"What makes you think you can go out tonight? You were grounded just last week for breaking curfew and you expect me to trust you now? Don't even think about it!"*

An environment conducive to experiencing appropriate *guilt* might look or sound like:

◆ *"Since you wore your sister's shirt without permission, you need to confess your wrong and then pay for the shirt to be dry cleaned."* (As part of the consequences for family conflict, each person is encouraged to confess, seek forgiveness, and make restitution—i.e. replace damaged property, clean sister's room, earn extra allowance to pay back $$, etc. The subject is then dropped.)

◆ *"Because you chose to wait until 5:00 to start cleaning your room, you will have to miss some of the pool party. Remember, the rule is ... when your room is clean, then you can play."*

◆ *"When you talk loudly in church, other people can't hear the preacher. He is saying important words to help us understand and experience what the Bible says, so it's important to be quiet."*

◆ *"Mommy is feeling upset right now, but it is not because I'm upset with you. I am worried about "adult things." I'll be fine—Dad and I will talk about it tonight."*

As you consider the above, write your reflections and any desired changes:

Because I need to stop contributing to an environment of condemnation, it is important that I . . .

_____

_____

_____

_____

_____

_____

Apply the principles

Think about a recent time when your son or daughter broke one of your rules or one of God's laws. How did you resolve the issue? Did you provide a way of restitution and reconciliation? The following steps provide a guide to help your children deal with feelings of guilt.

1. **Help the child name the offense:** "What rule was broken?"

_____

_____

    (For example: "*I was wrong to take the toy from the church.*" Or, "*I disobeyed you when I went to Tiffany's without asking.*")

If a child is unable to identify the broken rule, then simply state the offense for them. Leave out any character judgments or name calling (liar, foolish, thief, stupid). Name the offense in objective terms.

    (For example: "*It was wrong to take the toy from the church. That is stealing.*" Or, "*The rule is: Before you go to someone else's house after school, you must get permission.*" etc.)

2. **Identify the ways this offense has hurt other people.** How have others been hurt by the child's actions? How do they feel?

    I would lead my child in this discussion by saying . . .

_____

_____

    (For example: "*What do you think Andrew might have been feeling when you said those unkind words?*" Or, "*How do you think Carrie felt when she let you borrow her CD player and it was never returned?*")

3. **Confess to God, experiencing I John 1:9.**

Encourage your child to confess their offense to God and to ask His forgiveness. Depending upon the age of the child, you may want to pray together or suggest spending private time talking with God.

A prayer of confession for my child might sound like:

_____

_____

_____

(For example: "*God, I was wrong to take the toy from the church. I know that is stealing. I hurt you when I sin. It makes you sad when I do things that are wrong. Please forgive me.*")

4. Confess to others as needed, experiencing James 5:16. If the offense has wounded or offended other persons, encourage your child to verbalize a confession to these individuals as well.

I would encourage my child to confess to others by saying

_____

_____

_____

(For example: "I would like for you to apologize to Andrew for your unkind words. Your confession could sound like this: 'Andrew, I was wrong to call you names and say those ugly words. You probably felt sad. Will you forgive me?'" Or, "I would like for you to apologize to Carrie before bedtime this evening. When you share your confession by sure to include that you were wrong and acknowledge how she must have felt. I will check in with you tonight to see how it went.")

Apply the principles
Help your child empty feelings of condemnation.

Think about a recent time when your child has demonstrat-ed a fear of losing your love or a tendency to equate his worth with his behavior. Or, think about a recent time when your child has blamed himself for things he is not responsible.

My child recently demonstrated feelings of condemnation when

_____

_____

_____

("*Justin expresses feelings of condemnation when he con-stantly tells me he's sorry. His apologies seem to indicate that he's afraid of losing my approval or making me upset.*" Or "*Cara demonstrated feelings of condemnation when she prom-ised to be good if Daddy and I would stop fighting.*")

1. **Initiate meeting the needs for affection, acceptance, and attention.** Be sure to communicate that your child is worth having the needs met.

   I could meet my child's need for affection and acceptance by

   _____

   _____

   (Giving frequent hugs and "I love you's." Or telling her there's nothing she can do to lose my love.)

   I could meet my child's need for attention by

   _____

   _____

   ("prioritizing his school events and getting involved in sports activities." Or "reading the same novel that he's reading for English and then spending time discussing the book- just to be able to share in his world.")

2. **Give comfort.** You will want to communicate this comfort in the following ways:

Share words of comfort over how your child's sin has hurt him (if sin or disobedience is involved). For example: *"I hurt for you. I know how hard it has been to miss the football games and the chance to be with your friends."* (The child knows that missing games is the consequence for inappropriate behavior at previous games.) Or *"I feel sad when I see you in time out. I know how hard it is to sit quietly instead of getting to play outside."* (The child clearly understands that the time out is a consequence for disobedience.)

My child might need to hear these comforting words (over how his sin has hurt him):

_____

_____

Share words of comfort when no sin or disobedience is involved. Share comfort over painful events that have happened to the child and how sad you are that the child blames herself. For example: *"I know our fighting makes you feel scared and sad. I'm sad that our fighting hurts you. My heart is also sad to hear that you think that Mommy and Daddy's fights are because of you. I want you to know that our fighting is not your fault. We love you. There's nothing you can do to make us love you more or love you less."*

For example: *"Sweetheart, I feel so sad when I think about how hurtful it has been to see your mom/dad break her/his promises over and over again. I know it was especially hurtful on the days when you were looking forward to his/her visits and he/she never came. But even more than that, it breaks my heart to know that you blame yourself. I feel so much sadness knowing that you've concluded this is your fault."*

My child needs to hear these comforting words (over the painful event and assuming blame for the event):

_____

_____

_____

3. **Separate your children's worth from their behavior.** This might look like the following:

Implement consequences for disobedience and then refrain from bringing up the offense again.

Give names to the offense rather than the person. It would be appropriate to tell a child that lying is wrong, but not appropriate to tell a child she is a liar.

After discipline or consequences have occurred, communicate your love for your child, but your dislike for the behavior. Emphasize that God also separates our worth from our behavior (See Romans 5:8).

One of the changes I want to make in helping my child separate his worth from his behavior is

_____
_____
_____
_____

(For example: "*I need to implement consequences and then let the issue drop. I have a habit of reminding my children of their past mistakes.*" Or "*I need to reassure Timothy of my love for him after a time of discipline. I might say, 'Timothy, Mommy doesn't like it when you hit your sister. It's wrong to hurt others. But I want you to know that Mommy loves you. That will never change.'*")

4. **Encourage your child to express gratitude for God's care and concern on her behalf.** These expressions of gratitude help solidify a child's worth to the Heavenly Father. This might look like:

◆ Keeping a family diary of all the blessings God has given to each person.

◆ Thanking God for specific demonstrations of care at each family meal.

◆ Drawing pictures of the ways God cares for each family member.

◆ Writing God a letter thanking Him for His provision and care.

Knock, Knock . . . Who's There?
Ministering to Your Child's Aloneness

The emotions we've described in this chapter—hurt, anger, fear, guilt, and condemnation—can be overwhelming for a child. Sometimes when we feel overwhelmed, we also feel alone. Remember how God ministered to Adam's aloneness? He gave him another human—Eve. In like manner, He has given your children—you! God wants to minister to your child's aloneness through you. This is not to say that they won't need times of solitude, but there's a difference between feeling alone and solitude.

Yes, it's a cruel world and in many respects you can't change that. But you can provide a safe haven, a protected environment for them in which emotions can be safely shared. Every child will experience hurt in life. Therefore, every child needs a mom and a dad who will be there to help heal the inevitable hurts so they don't fester into rage, paralyzing fear, or condemnation. As you do so, you'll also be pointing them beyond yourself—to the God of all comfort and a God who is love!

Let's communicate to our children: *"I know life can be tough, but I want you to know I'm here to help you. Let's find a way to use these difficult feelings to build relationships instead of destroying them."* Every day seek to be a healer in the lives of your children.

Scripture Reflection and Prayer

"Let no unwholesome word proceed from your mouth, but only such a word as is good for edification according to the need of the moment, that it may give grace to those who hear." (Ephesians 4:29)

Reflect on this verse and write your thoughts regarding how living out this Scripture in your home can impact your ability to help your child deal with painful emotions:

_____

_____

_____

Express a prayer to God, asking Him for his wisdom and sensitivity in enabling you to speak edifying words to your children:

Dear God, I want to stop all unwholesome words and instead build up my children according to what they need. Please help me to . . .

_____

_____

_____

Special Thoughts for Single Parents

The subject of painful emotions reminds us that "It is not good to be alone," (Genesis 2:18). If we try to deal with our own painfully full "emotional cup" alone, we will tend to "spill out" unproductively on our children. We will be more likely to blame, criticize, minimize, or give logic in response to their emotion.

Do you have at least one person with whom you can be honest and genuine, even concerning your own sadness, anger, fears, guilt, and condemnation? Does this person know how to help you genuinely resolve these difficult emotions? If not, seek to develop a mutually satisfying friendship for yourself so that you might not be so alone. You will then have more to give to your children!

Another significant emotional challenge may involve dealing with a child's disappointments because of an ex-spouse's behavior. Avoid blaming or criticizing your ex-spouse. But also avoid "sugar-coating" the issue. Your children need adults who will face the truth with them, helping them to realize that sometimes adults, even parents, do things that hurt them. Then they need for you to give comfort for that hurt: *"It saddens me that you were hurt this weekend because I care about you. I love you, and it hurts me that you were hurt."*

Special Thoughts for Blended Families

As a step-parent, how do you feel when your step-child misses his or her biological parent? Do you feel threatened? Jealous? Or compassionate? Children need permission to talk about missing the other parent. They need an environment that is safe enough to express those emotions.

Children also need to know that they can rely on you to take responsibility for what you can control—your own responses. Your children may experience two very different emotional "environments" when they move from one household to another. It's important to first provide a safe and secure emotional "refuge" in your home. Then, even though you can't control the other environment, you can be empathetic and comforting of the pain that may be experienced there.

Experiencing Biblical Truth

We can use an acrostic for experiencing Biblical truths as we deal with the emotion of anger. This acrostic could be helpful as we deal with our own anger or someone else's anger.

A— *Acknowledge the anger.*

Ephesians 4:26 affirms that anger will occur at times but it also stresses the importance of what we do with our anger. Stop and reflect on the last time you felt angry.

◆ Briefly describe the circumstances which prompted your angry feelings.

I felt angry when

_____

_____
_____

(For example: *"I felt angry when John came home two hours later than we had discussed. I needed his help watching the kids so that I could prepare for my Bible Study. Or, I felt angry when my manager gave a promotion to a less experienced, less qualified co-worker. My manager had been encouraging me to work extra hours so that I would be a "sure thing" for the upcoming promotion.")*

◆ Briefly share this event with your partner and invite your partner to do the same.

N— *Notice the relationships.*

◆ After each person has finished sharing, partners then "reflect" back to each other the feeling and content of what was just shared— paying particular attention to the relationships involved in the situation "Reflecting back" means telling in your own words what your partner has just shared. (This "reflecting back" also communicates acceptance and understanding.)

It sounds like you felt angry because . .

_____

_____

_____

(For example: *"It sounds like you were really mad because we had agreed upon a plan and I didn't follow through with my part of the deal. You were counting on me. Or, So, you were angry because you felt this co-worker didn't deserve the promotion. You were especially angry because of the extra hours and because your boss had led you to believe the promotion was yours."*)

G— *Get to the more tender feeling through giving each other a "gentle answer"*

◆ Each of you give a "gentle answer" (Proverbs 15:1) to your partner. Your response should seek to identify a tender emotion that might be underneath the anger. Tender emotions might include: (hurt, disappointment, sad, afraid, alone, etc.) Your "gentle answer" might sound like:

_____

_____

_____

For example: *"I'm wondering if you were also feeling hurt and unsupported. When I didn't come home on time you might have felt hurt because the promise was broken. You might have felt unsupported because your preparation for Bible Study is really important to you."*

For example: *"I sense that you might also have felt disappointed, unappreciated, deceived, or taken for granted. You were excited about the possibility of this promotion and had been led to believe it was yours. You not only must have been disappointed when you didn't get the promotion, but were questioning your boss's sincerity. You must have also felt unappreciated and taken for granted when a less experienced person got the job."*

Respond to your partner with these words: *I know you were angry, but I'm wondering if you might also have felt hurt that . . .*

_____

_____

_____

◆ Then give your partner a chance to confirm these tender feelings or to edit them. You might ask, *"Am I on target here?"* Or, *"Have I heard you well?"*

E— *Experience and express care.*

◆ After each partner has confirmed or edited their "gentle answers" and each feels understood, respond with expressions of care.

If your partner expressed hurt, then share words of comfort and feelings of sadness for them.

If you were a part of hurting your spouse or partner, then make an appropriate confession.

If your partner expressed fear, then share your commitment to walk through this with them.

R— *Respond wisely.*

Once you have acknowledged your anger and expressed the more tender emotions and experienced care, you are in a position to respond wisely, experiencing the truths of Ephesians 4:26-27 and 4:31-32. You can now prevent the sun from going down on your anger and the devil from having an opportunity to poison your relationships (Eph. 4:26-27). You are also now in a place to be able to "get rid" your anger (Eph. 4:31) through forgiveness (Eph. 4:32).

Homework For Our Homes

Make opportunities this week to discuss emotions. Set aside time at meals, bed time or after homework is done to tell stories about feelings. On one night tell stories about a time when you felt excited, thrilled, or happy. The next night tell stories about a time when you felt hurt, sad, disappointed, or discouraged. Choose a different theme for each night. You'll also want to expand your family's feeling vocabulary by choosing feelings that may be less familiar.

Parents will want to tell stories first. Tell your story and be sure to include lots of interesting details and plenty of feeling words. Make sure the length of your story is appropriate for the attention span of your child. You'll also want to think of a "feeling story" that occurred at about the same age as one of your children. If you have a seven-year-old, try to tell a story about the time when you were seven. If you have an adolescent, tell a story about from your teen years.

Finally, encourage your children to tell their own stories. Listen without interruption or correction. Don't correct a child who doesn't get the facts just right or her version isn't quite accurate. Just focus on understanding how your child felt in the moment of her story.

As each child finishes, parents will want to respond emotionally. If your child shares a positive emotion, then celebrate with them, "*Oh yes, that was exciting! I know that was fun for you!*" Or, "*I'm so glad that happened to you. That was terrific!*" If your child shares a painful feeling, then share your sadness about that event, "*I know that day was hard for you. I felt sad too.*" Or, "*Oh I know that must have hurt. I'm sorry that happened.*"

End your story telling time with a short prayer. Thank God for giving us emotions and for revealing Biblical guidelines for handling our emotions. Finally, ask God to use your feelings to draw you closer to Him and to one another.

Chapter 7

— ■ —

CHILDREN AS YOUR
DEAREST DISCIPLES
(HOW CHILD DISCIPLINE MUST EXPRESS
GENUINE DISCIPLESHIP)

In this workbook, we have strongly asserted that every person has two challenges, two critical issues, which must be addressed: Every person is "fallen"—no one is perfect—we all commit wrongs (Romans 3:23; 6:23). And we all have struggles with being alone.

The implication for parenting? The dual challenge of properly responding to both challenges in the lives of our children, as well as dealing with our own fallenness and aloneness!

This chapter is about child discipline—responding to our children's misbehavior—their expressions of fallenness—from a "parenting with intimacy" perspective. But before we present specifically all that might entail, we must assert the following:

Child discipline is done a great injustice when removed from the larger framework of discipleship!

What do we mean by discipleship? Let's consider this first through the eyes of Donald, a pastor friend of David Ferguson.

Donald had struggled throughout his ministry with overwork. He and his wife were together on that difficulty in his life—no disagreement there. He was always at the church, visiting church members in their homes, or engaged in denominational commitments. He had tried to change, even shedding tears on many occasions over his compulsion to work and the neglect of his family.

This dilemma prompted an in-depth discussion with David Ferguson. One day, with tears streaming down his cheeks, he asked David, "Why? Why won't I go home? I know my family needs me."

As they talked, he began to pour out his heart. Toward the end of their time together, Donald said, "You know, I think a major reason why I don't go home is I'm afraid. I'm afraid that I don't know how to be a father. I know my children need me, but I'm not sure I know what they need. I'm not sure I know how to give it to them. I feel adequate preaching, managing my staff, and discipling my congregation, but I don't feel adequate with my own children."

So, Donald invested himself, sometimes to the point of exhaustion, in discipling his congregation. All the while his dearest disciples, his own children, were neglected. Donald's not alone in this struggle. Many parents—fathers and mothers from many walks of life, feel inadequate with their own children. They direct their energies toward building into the lives of others first, leaving the "leftovers" to those at home.

Your children are your dearest *disciples.* Paraphrasing a familiar Bible passage, *what profit would it be if we gained the whole world ...* and lost our children? This is an alarming possibility but an all too common reality.

In one of the largest research projects of church-attending youth ever undertaken, noted author and speaker Josh McDowell teamed up with researcher George Barna to conduct the extensive "Right from Wrong" campaign (McDowell, 1993). Over and over in issues such as lying, cheating, pornography, drugs, and premarital sex, parents were failing to pass on Bible-centered values to their children. The alarm was sounded for a multi-year campaign, enlisting thousands of churches and Christian ministries, and hundreds of thousands of parents to focus on one battle cry—**Protect your child** from being **captured by the culture.** Our dearest disciples have missed the Biblical values we've hoped to impart, so who do we look to for answers? We look to the Savior!

Jesus Christ stands without comparison in countless ways—His virgin birth, sinless life, sacrificial death, and miraculous resurrection, just to name a few. But among the most practically relevant to parenting with intimacy is His uniqueness in propagating His message. Other so-called "religious leaders" might establish great schools or generate voluminous writings—but not Jesus! He simply trained disciples! He did not build great monuments, structures, or libraries—He invested His life in the lives of a few people. This is still the secret of truly propagating the Gospel. Men and women become disciples of Christ and then are used by God to disciple others. The essence of Christ's call to make disciples is found in this proverb: "I may impress people from a distance but I can only impact them up close!"

The Greek word for "disciple" simply means "a learner, one who is taught, a follower." Christ's goal was to impart His very life to His disciples. To that end, He shared His conflicts, joys, prayer life, and His relationship with the Father. He thus became the "context" or setting for His own teaching. This is the essence of discipleship. The apostle Paul affirmed the importance of discipleship when he said, *"We were pleased to impart to you not only the gospel of God but also our own very lives"* (1 Thessalonians 2:8).

Mothers often lament having to put their desires to be involved in a discipleship ministry on a back burner until their children are at least old enough to be in school all day. Fathers often look to the workplace or within the church for men to disciple, as Donald did. What if fathers and mothers in "training up their children in the way they should go" saw as their priority the "discipling" of their own children—modeling for them a life of Christlikeness and then spending the time and love necessary to see this Christlikeness reproduced in their children? After all, how difficult is it to lead a consistent life in front of someone you meet with once a week for an hour? In contrast, the challenge to live out your faith twenty-four hours a day with your children is one guaranteed to keep your feet to the fire!

And Dads, Ephesians 6:4 exhorts us to "bring up our children in the **training** and **instruction** of the Lord." "Training" in this verse means *training by actions*—modeling and demonstrating how to live. "Instruction" here means *verbal direction*—explaining and literally "putting in the child's heart and mind" God's truth and wisdom.

Parents are called upon to impart their very lives to their children and, by doing so, impact them positively for Christ.

True discipleship lies at the very heart of "success" in the Christian home.

So where does child discipline fit into all of this? How can we respond effectively to our children's misbehavior and still be lovingly "imparting our lives" to them?

In this chapter, we outline six ingredients for effective discipline which involve extending and applying principles of discipleship to the challenge of dealing with our children's misbehavior. In so doing we will continue to grow and develop in our "parenting with intimacy," reflecting God's concern for and provision for both fallenness and aloneness!

STOP AND CONSIDER

How did Christ transfer His message to a few disciples? List some of the *methods* He used to impart His life to these few who, in turn, turned the world upside down. (For instance: "*He shared everyday life events with them; He shared His ideas, plans, and pain with them.*")

_____

_____

_____

Reflect on 2 Timothy 2:2 *"And the things which you have heard from me in the presence of many witnesses, these entrust to faithful men, who will be able to teach others also."* Write your thoughts on how this relates to parenting with intimacy:

_____

_____

_____

Six Ingredients for
Disciplining Our Children

Although children may not recognize it, discipline is part of parents' expression of unconditional love. It represents their willingness to do whatever is in the best interest of their children, even though a parent's effort to discipline might not be appreciated.

Have you ever had this experience? You're sitting at the breakfast table enjoying that first cup of coffee and reading the newspaper. Your daughter (or son) sits down next to you, excitedly pulls the paper from your hands and gushes, "Dad, I just want to tell you...thanks so much for grounding me last night. I realize that I am self-centered, materialistic, and narcissistic, and that you were only doing what was in my best interest when you refused to let me buy everything I wanted at the mall. You and Mom are doing a great job with me. I'm so lucky to have you as parents!" You're still waiting, aren't you! If we're honest, though, we'd have to admit that we do halfway expect this kind of glowing feedback from our children and then are offended when it doesn't come. Unconditional love says, "I'm committed to doing whatever is in your best interests, whether you agree with me or not—and whether or not you appreciate me."

Let's look at six key ingredients in this process of disciplining your children.

(1) Intimacy

Intimate relationships—knowing our children and letting them know us for the purpose of experiencing care—are the foundation for all effective discipline. Just as surely as bread without yeast will never rise, trying to discipline a child in an environment lacking intimacy will be disastrous. There must be a foundation of love and friendship. Remember the Heavenly Father's example: He provides intimate love first, then discipline is an appropriate and necessary expression of that love (See Hebrews 12:6).

Various "imbalances" may exist. Sometimes parents may exhibit high "strictness" (control) but with too little experience of knowing and caring. Other times parents may be highly permissive (not enough control). This is sometimes mistakenly viewed as intimacy when really it may be neglectful uninvolvement!.

In some homes, the "Tough Parent-Easy Parent" philosophy of discipline may be played out: "You (*mother*) give them the love; I'll (*father*) give them the discipline." Wrong! Love and discipline must fit together like a hand fits in a glove. Each parent needs to be involved in both. Children benefit greatly when they see that the same hands that discipline them also love and comfort them—just like the Heavenly Father.

When discipline is administered in an atmosphere in which there is no intimacy or too little intimacy, children will often grow up to resent the discipline (and the discipliner) and a root of bitterness may develop. Children can end up thinking, "There is this stranger who seems to enter my life only when I'm doing something wrong and punishes me, and I resent that." There's possibly no quicker way to *"provoke a child to anger"* than to discipline without the foundation of intimacy (Eph. 6:4).

Developing intimacy with your child requires an investment of time, but it will yield monumental results. Remember, your "disciples" can be most effectively impacted through intimate relationships with both you and the Savior.

STOP AND CONSIDER

Stop and consider your level of *intimacy* with each child. To what extent are your children experiencing mutual knowing for the purpose of caring involvement?

Child: *Circle the words which best describe your relationship:*

	I know him/her.	He/she knows me.	He/she consistently experiences my care.
————————	I know him/her.	He/she knows me.	He/she consistently experiences my care.
————————	I know him/her.	He/she knows me.	He/she consistently experiences my care.
————————	I know him/her.	He/she knows me.	He/she consistently experiences my care.
————————	I know him/her.	He/she knows me.	He/she consistently experiences my care.

What steps could you take to deepen intimacy with each child? Write your reflections below: (For instance, "*Lately, it seems to take a few hours for Timothy to warm up to me. My frequent business trips obviously affect our level of intimacy. I'll request trips that are in-state only. When I do have to travel, I'll plan to do something fun with Timothy before I go, and then we'll schedule some fun "reunion" activity when I return.*")

———————————————————————————————

———————————————————————————————

———————————————————————————————

The second ingredient of effective "discipline as discipleship" is:

(2) Instruction (What to do)

Children need to be clearly told what is expected of them. We ought not expect them to "read our minds!" Help them understand the "big picture," that the goal is not just compliance on their part but helping them learn to be responsible for themselves. Then make sure the rules and expectations are clear and consistent. As we improve the quality of our instruction, let's strive to:

1. Be clear: Tell your child specifically and precisely what you would like done and the necessary time frame. The age and development of a child may require that the instructions be broken down into smaller pieces. For example, a clear instruction might sound like, "Jonathan, please take your clothes up stairs to your room and put them in your drawers. I'd like for you to do that before we sit down for dinner."

Jonathan's young age may require that his parent give the instructions in separate steps. For instance, "Jonathan, I'd like for you to take your basket of clothes up to your room and set it by your dresser." (After Jonathan has completed this task, the next instruction is given:) "Now, I want you to put the clean socks and pajamas in the top drawer, and the rest of the clothes in the bottom drawer. Lay them neatly inside."

2. Be positive: Express expectations in a positive form, whenever possible. Use polite, firm language and remove any put downs. For example, "Please take your clothes to the laundry room" will be more effective than "Quit leaving your clothes all over the floor! You're such a slob!"

3. Be concise: Be brief as you give your child instructions. Children get lost in a lecture.

A special word of caution is warranted at this juncture. Be careful not to convey condemnation to your children. Sadly, statements like these are sometimes made by frustrated parents, "If you can't straighten yourself out, you're never going to amount to anything," or "Can't you do anything right?" It's eerie how often these "prophetic" condemning statements come to fruition.

Instead, meet their need for encouragement by saying things like, "Your mom and I believe you can handle this." Reassure them that you'll be available if they need help and that they can always come back to home plate for a visit with the umpires!

Stop and Consider

Stop and consider the *Instruction* ingredient of discipline. Indicate the phrases which would be most true of you. (Check with your spouse, a friend, or an older child if you're not sure!)

___ I take time to instruct my children.
___ Instructions are seldom given.
___ My children should know what I expect from them by now—
      I shouldn't have to tell them what to do.
___ My instructions are given in a positive way.
___ My instructions are given in a critical way.
___ My children need to be better "mind-readers!"
___ I usually express my instructions in a sentence or two.
___ I may sometimes over-express my instructions—either too
      many words or too many different instructions.

Write about any changes you'd like to make: (For instance, "*I know Anna must think I'm on her case all the time. I'll give her clear, positive instructions. I'll be less critical, and hopefully Anna will feel more success by completing more manageable tasks.*")

_____

_____

_____

_____

_____

The third ingredient in effective discipline:

(3) Training (showing them how to do it)

Most parents will agree that the three most dreaded words on Christmas Eve are "Some Assembly Required." As you sit down with the box, you tip it upside down, dumping all 355 parts on the floor, and proceed to correctly put each piece in the proper place with no instructions—right? Hardly! Why, even with the instruction manual, it often requires several attempts before some semblance of victory can be claimed. Why, then, would we expect our children, without help, to know not only *what* they should do but *how* they should do it?

The best training for your disciples is through your **example**! (This is actually what the word "discipline" [NASB] or "training" [NIV] means in Ephesians 6:4.) Our children are watching when we speak respectfully or rudely, whether or not we help around the house, and whether or not we remain gentle when provoked. Look carefully at what we're modeling. If we're trying to teach our child to be polite and listen without interrupting, we'll need to model these behaviors as we talk to our spouses, church members, co-workers and other family members.

Training may require **hands-on** demonstration with the child. For example, "Take out the trash" may sound simple to us but not to an eight-year-old. Proper training for this task might include: (1) find all the small trash containers around the house; (2) empty them; (3) replace trash liners; (4) return trash containers to their previous locations; (5) take larger trash bag to the sidewalk. *Show them how, then do it together, then turn them loose to do it on their own!*

Stop and Consider

Stop and consider: In what areas does each child need additional training?

As you consider each one, what "training" from you might be helpful—either better training through your improved example or "hands-on" training as you come alongside and show them how. Write your thoughts here: (For instance, "*I need to show Alexis what I mean when I say, 'Please set the table.' That means: set out four placements and napkins; put a knife, fork, and spoon on each placement, etc. We'll do it together two or three times, then I'll let her try it on her own.*" Or "*I need to train all the kids in how to handle telephone calls. I must improve my example in things like: speaking respectfully, taking messages and handling tele-marketers.*")

Child _____
Training is needed in this area _____
I could model this in my own life by . . . Or I could demonstrate how to . . . by . . _____

_____

_____

Child _____
Training is needed in this area _____
I could model this in my own life by . . . Or I could demonstrate how to . . . by . . _____

_____

_____

Child _____
Training is needed in this area _____
I could model this in my own life by . . . Or I could demonstrate how to . . . by . . _____

_____

_____

The fourth ingredient:

(4) Warning (Setting and expressing consequences)

Effective discipline must include an element of warning. How should warnings be expressed?

1. Communicate an impending consequence if the behavior is not stopped or task completed.

Parents frequently tell their kids to stop doing something or to start doing something. Sometimes, when the kids resist, complain, dawdle, or ignore the directive, parents may repeat the directive, possibly with an increasingly louder tone of voice: "I told you to do it AND I MEAN NOW!!!"

What else may be needed? The kids likely need a clear statement about what will happen if instructions are not followed or what conditions must be met before a privilege is allowed: "I asked you to put away the game before you get any more toys out. If you do, then you can go ahead and set up the trains. But if you don't, you won't be allowed to get anything else out."

What types of consequences should we consider?

It's important to have a repertoire of consequences which are age-appropriate. Your consequences might include:

a. **Natural Consequences:** letting children experience consequences which result from their behaviors. These are consequences which occur "naturally"—parents don't have to intervene to make them happen.

◆ Keeping a toddler safe is important, but sometimes it's wise to "back off" from repeated warnings and, for example, occasionally let him bump his head under the coffee table. He'll soon learn not to raise up while crawling underneath.

◆ Remind a teenage driver about his expired inspection sticker only once. Then allow that teenager to experience the natural consequence of receiving and paying for a traffic ticket.

b. **Logical Consequences**: implementing consequences such as "time out," restitution, or loss of privileges. These consequences do require parental intervention to make them happen. They are "logical" to the extent that the "consequence fits the misdeed."

◆ "Time out" (for children ages 2 to 8 or 9) involves being required to sit in a chair doing nothing for a specified period of time, usually one minute per year of age. A cooking timer can be helpful to let everyone know that the appropriate time has elapsed.

◆ Restitution might involve, "Brad, if you damage the back of the car seat by kicking it, you will do extra chores in order to earn money for repairs."

◆ Loss of privileges might sound like, "Paige, if you receive one more speeding ticket, in addition to paying the fine, you will lose the privilege of driving the car for three months."

Logical consequences may also include **ignoring or choosing not to respond to certain** behaviors. You might want to ignore a child's whining or complaining. Or, you could choose to respond when the behavior has subsided: "Ashley, as soon as you stop whining, I will talk with you."

What about **spanking?** We recommend that spanking be reserved as a rare consequence for absolute defiance or issues of personal safety (electrical outlets, crossing the street, etc.) Spanking should only be implemented with younger children, typically between the ages of 18 - 24 months and 8 - 9 years of age.

2. **Acknowledge the desires and feelings of a child.**

Acknowledging the desires and feelings of a child communicates sensitivity and awareness of a child's world. This does not mean that a parent allows a child's feelings and desires to dictate consequences or determine decisions. Acknowledging feelings simply assures children that parents care about them and their feelings even if consequences occur that they don't like.

Acknowledging feelings or desires might sound like, "Meredith, I know you'd like to keep playing outside, but our rule is: You can play outside until it gets dark." Or "Nathan, I know it's important for you fit in with your friends and you hate to be 'different.' But in our home, those kind of movies are not acceptable."

3. **State specifically what's expected so that whether the child responds properly can be measured.**

Be **specific** as you communicate your warning. Your warning might be stated in this form: *When . . then . . .* or *If . . . then . . . .* For instance: "When your homework is finished then you can ride your bike." "You can borrow the car after the lawn is mowed." "If you keep throwing the blocks, we will have to put them up."

The warnings should also be **measurable**, meaning that any reasonable observer could determine whether the standard or instruction has been met: the toys have been picked up and put into their proper places or they have not—no room for argument about whether it was done or whether it was done in the appropriate time frame.

4. **Express consequences the parent is willing to enforce.**

Make sure your warning is something you are committed to carry through. Giving multiple threats to spank or send a child to "time out" but then rarely following through only teaches a child to "tune out." He begins to learn, "I don't have to comply with Mommy's instruction until she's really angry." Or, "I don't have to do what Daddy says until he uses 'that tone of voice.'"

Similarly, if you give a child a "when / then" warning—"When your room is clean then we can go ice skating"—be sure to keep your word. Only when the room is clean do we leave to take the child ice skating. Give your "disciples" the security of keeping your word.

Effective warnings helps to develop a predictable and secure home environment.

STOP AND CONSIDER

Stop and consider the *Warning* ingredient in your relationship with your children. How would you evaluate the "warning element" of your discipline? Circle the responses which you think best fit you.

1. My warnings communicate an upcoming consequence if the behavior is not stopped or task completed.

   Consistently   Occasionally   Seldom

2. I acknowledge the desires and feelings of my children.

   Consistently   Occasionally   Seldom

3. My warnings are specific and measurable.

   Consistently   Occasionally   Seldom

4. My warnings express consequences I am willing to enforce.

   Consistently   Occasionally   Seldom

What changes would you like to see made?

(For instance: "*I need to stop making threats that I don't plan to carry out. When Belinda acts up in McDonald's, I need to give her one positive warning. "You can play on the playground as long as you get along with the other kids."* or *"I need to make the boundaries and consequences clear for weekend activities. I'll decide on consequences for breaking curfew before the next weekend and discuss them with Alicia. This way, I won't get trapped into thinking up consequences in the "heat of the moment.'*)

_____

_____

_____

_____

The fifth ingredient in effective "parenting with intimacy" discipline is:

(5) Correction (implement consequences)

Correction should be implemented with self-control and firmness, and without anger. The consequences are not capricious or arbitrary; they have already been well thought out. The consequences have been discussed and agreed upon by both Mom and Dad (if both parents live at home). Single parents may want to discuss implementation of possible consequences with a trusted friend.

An important perspective for effective correction: we must distinguish between *discipline* and *punishment.*

Review the following chart contrasting discipline and punishment:

Discipline...Don't Punish

	Punishment	Discipline
Parent's Goal	Retribution and penalty	Develop responsibility and self-control
Parent's Attitude	Frustration, hostility, or rejection	Love; Concern for effect of misbehavior on child;
Parent's Emphasis	Current wrongs and past mistakes	Future—improved behavior and attitude
Child's Emotional Response	Anger Condemnation Fear	Security Gratitude
Child's Concept of God	God seeks to punish and is therefore to be avoided.	God loves and protects through discipline; He is available and worth knowing intimately.

STOP AND CONSIDER

Stop and consider these distinctions between discipline and punishment. Which elements of *true discipline* have you learned to incorporate? Which results do you see in the lives of your children? *Circle the descriptions which best fit you and your children. Then write further reflections below:*

_____

_____

_____

_____

Now write about any elements of punishment you see in your home and tell God what you'd like to see changed. (For instance, "*God, I don't want to punish Kevin in anger. I know my frustration level is short these days, but I don't want to crush his spirit. Change my attitude and response as I change from punishment to loving discipline.*")

_____

_____

_____

_____

_____

Now consider your most current recurring discipline issues for each of your children. What consequences need to be in place and enforced? What additional types of consequences might you want to consider?

_____

_____

_____

_____

Identify the most pressing discipline issue for each child. Then decide what consequences seem to be working and what additional consequences might be appropriate. Discuss any new plans with your spouse or friend:

Child _____ Current Discipline Issue:_____

_____

Consequence that is working:_____

_____

Consequence I would like to implement:_____

_____

_____

Child _____ Current Discipline Issue:_____

Consequence that is working:_____

Consequence I would like to implement:_____

_____

Child _____ Current Discipline Issue:_____

Consequence that is working:_____

Consequence I would like to implement:_____

_____

The final ingredient

(6) Reassurance of Your Unconditional Love and Acceptance

After you have corrected your child, communicate acceptance through touch, words, hugs, and other expressions of love. Your reassurance will communicate, "I'm displeased with your behavior, but I'm separating your behavior from your worth. I am committed to you and love you unconditionally. There's nothing you could ever *do* that would make me stop loving you."

Reassurance might include:
◆ Not reminding your child of past offenses: "Remember that time when you..."
◆ Demonstrating forgiveness (letting go of anger), rather than staying angry.
◆ Letting the consequence be the sufficient "payment" for the offense.
◆ Communicating your reassurance verbally and directly: "Mommy loves you and wants what's best for you."

◆ Non-verbal reassurances, such as a gentle hug after conse-quences have been completed and emotions are settled or rubbing your child's back when you tuck him in at night.

Your reassurance of unconditional love models the Heavenly Father's declaration of our worth to Him. *"Christ died for us,"* in spite of our behavior—*"while we were yet sinners"* (Romans 5:8).

At this point of the journey, parents can give children the security of knowing that no matter what they *do,* their parents will always love them. As they develop their concept of God, through the lens of how they see their earthly parents, the groundwork has been laid. Your children can rest securely in the arms of a God who loves them with a love that is perfect and complete. Do not minimize the impact of this step of reas-surance. Your child will reap what you sow—now, and for gen-erations to come.

STOP AND CONSIDER

Stop and consider how you give reassurance of uncondi-tional love as part of responding to your children's misbehavior. Write about any needed changes below: (For instance: "*I need to give reassurance to Melanie. She knows that lying about her weekend plans was wrong and that her discipline was appro-priate, but I never reassured her of my love. I need to initiate a hug and an evening bike ride together.*" Or "*I need to tell Cameron that I was angry with what he did but I love him and I'm committed to working it out.*")

_____

_____

_____

_____

_____

_____

Why Else Do Children Misbehave?
Look for the Needs
Beneath the Deeds

Even with faithful, consistent, loving implementation of these six discipline ingredients, there will be times when your children will misbehave. It's a fact of life! Remember the Zaccheus Principle we discussed in chapter three? Let's explore that concept in more depth, looking for the "needs beneath the deeds."

Children, like their parents, will do wrong because of their sin nature. It is their "fallenness" or lack of relating intimately with their Creator that produces misbehavior. No one has to teach a child to lie or rebel against his parents' wishes. A child is born with a fallen nature that causes him to sin. Therefore as parents, we are reminded of our role in the life of each child—to point them toward an intimate, transforming relationship with God. We must then address a child's fallenness by inviting each child into a personal relationship with God, while at the same time implementing appropriate discipline whenever misbehavior occurs.

As discussed before, a child's misbehavior requires appropriate discipline—but don't stop there! There may also be times when children's unmet needs have left them more vulnerable to sin. A child's unmet need for attention my leave him more vulnerable to his sin nature—concluding that negative attention is better than none at all. A child's unmet need for affection may leave her more vulnerable to her sin nature—concluding that inappropriate affection is better than going without.

Parents need to take the time to discern all the factors contributing to their children's misbehavior. It's very easy to notice children's wrong behavior and immediately discipline them only based on their actions. But this may not tell the full story. It is wise also to look beyond the misbehavior and try to identify any underlying feelings, thoughts and unmet needs.

Although parents don't cause children to misbehave, problems can become worse if parents do not seek to understand their child's needs and feelings and respond as *adults*! As parents respond to the needs of a child, they role model Christ's love and point the child toward the "God who supplies all your needs" (see Phillipians 4:19). This will prepare them to one day consider the eternal significance of needing to relate intimately not only to parents but also to their Creator through His Son Jesus Christ. As you're faced with daily parenting decisions, ask yourself, "What would Jesus do?"

"If any of you lacks wisdom, let him ask of God, who gives to all men generously and without reproach, and it will be given to him" (James 1:5).

STOP AND CONSIDER

Stop and consider the last time your child misbehaved. What need might have been underneath the deed? What unmet need might have made him more vulnerable to "acting out" his fallenness? Write your ideas here:

_____

_____

_____

_____

_____

(For instance: *"I see how the power struggles with Luke over getting dressed are really evidence of his need for my attention. He needs for me to take more initiative to play with him."* Or *"Jordan's angry outburst was really an indication of his hurt. I know I disappointed him when I broke my promise. He was counting on me attending his concert and my absence and indifference hurt him. He needed my attention first, and then my confession when the promise was broken."*)

What might you have done additionally to meet this need and possibly avoid the misbehavior?

_____

_____

_____

_____

(For instance: *"I could have stayed calm and let Luke know that as soon as he got dressed, I would play puzzles with him. I could have put the puzzles out of reach until I saw Luke comply with my request. I would have been controlling myself and the consequences and setting firm limits. This would have also met his need for security (defining the limits and boundaries). He may not have liked my responses, but it might have avoided the huge battle of getting dressed."* Or *"I could have met Jordan's need for attention and entered his world this weekend. My physical presence at his concert and by showing interest in his music could have prevented his disappointment. His disappointment turned to anger and these feelings contributed to his outburst on Sunday when I asked him to go to the store for me. He needed me to prioritize his event and be more involved with him."*)

Special Thoughts for Single Parents

Discipline for a single parent can at times be overwhelming. Having to face the challenge of avoiding the extremes of either harshness or permissiveness can be even more difficult when attempted alone.

As a single parent, it may be particularly easy to fall into the trap of permissiveness. When we encounter the pain associated with divorce, death or separation, there may be the mistaken tendency not to set limits with your child. You may find yourself not wanting to say "no" for fear of inflicting more hurt. But a loving parent is one that sets clear limits that give the child a sense of security. You will want to communicate to your child: "The family relationship may be different, but I am still the parent and committed to doing what is in your best interest."

Special Thoughts for Blended Families

Do any of your children spend time in another household besides yours? Recognize that you cannot control two households, but you can create a consistent environment for children when they are in your home. Try to identify and affirm any similarities between the two homes and strive to increase them.

Also realize that part of your job as parents and stepparents will be to help your children deal productively with the differences. The rules of one home may be different from the other. One home may be more permissive and the other more strict. Discuss these differences with your children and together think of ways to accommodate both. Also discuss your expectations for your children with your partner, so the two of you will be united. Are your expectations age-appropriate? Are the important issues kept important with the "not-so-important" expectations negotiable?

Finally, are you approachable on the subject of inconsistencies? Do your children have the freedom to tell you when they sense areas of unfairness? Are you willing to hear their frustrations over seemingly different expectations for biological children and stepchildren? Be proactive about approachability. Initiate these types of conversations, and give your children the chance to share any of the ways they think they are being treated unfairly.

Experiencing Biblical Truth: Courageous Confessions

After working through this and other chapters, have you identified any needs which have gone unmet for your child? Have there been times when your child has needed attention and was neglected or needed comfort and but felt alone? Have there been times when you missed meeting the need for security and your child felt uncertain and anxious? Have you identified any of these hurtful methods: discipline in anger; sarcasm; absence; neglect; dismissive tone of voice; not meeting emotional needs of appreciation, affection, or approval; punishing rather than disciplining; comparison, criticism, favoritism, or extreme conflict between adults? Have there been any ways in which you might have hurt your child?

Most likely, all of us would have to answer yes to at least one of the questions above? Why, you say? Since there are no perfect parents, hurt is inevitable. Just as we mentioned in earlier chapters, **our motives** as parents may be genuine love and concern. However, **our methods** may sometimes hurt our children. Since hurt is an inevitable reality in our families, we must know how to deal with the hurt and heal the painful emotions.

The following experiential exercises are designed to help us live out the Biblical principles of I John 1:9 and James 5:16. Doing these verses enable us to experience confession and forgiveness within our family relationships.

1. **Stop and consider ways in which you might have caused hurt in the life of your child.** John 16:8 tells us that God's Spirit is able to bring to mind any areas that need our confession, so ask Him to reveal these areas to you. Ask God to reveal to you the specific ways that you have caused pain for each child. Ask the Heavenly Father to bring to your mind the ways in which you have "missed the mark" as a parent.

   Ask God to reveal any times you may have been: selfish, insensitive, disrespectful, verbally or physically abusive, rejecting, unforgiving, unsupportive, inattentive, unloving, unapproachable, or critical.

   Ask God to help you admit: any times you may have focused on deeds and missed important needs of your child, any times you may have concentrated on the negative memories associated with your child rather than celebrated the positive, any times that your own childhood pain got in the way of your ability to be a parent, any times you may have disciplined harshly and out of anger, any times you may have broken promises or had wrong priorities.

   Spend several minutes quiet before the Lord.

2. **List the things that God brings to your mind by completing this sentence:**

I have hurt _____ *by my . . .*
         (child's name)

(For example: "*I have hurt Ashley by my unforgiveness. I have been unwilling to let go of mistakes she's made with the car. I have continued to hurt her by bringing up these mistakes in front of her friends and making fun of her ability to drive.*" Or, "*I have hurt Trevor by my harsh and angry words. I have called him names and cursed at him. I know my yelling and screaming have scared him.*")

_____

_____

_____

_____

3.   God considers our "missing the mark" (actions, words, non-actions) as sin, and it is for our sin that Christ had to die (Isaiah 53:5). It was because of our criticism, sharp tongue, unforgiveness and neglect that our Savior was sent to the cross. What feelings does this truth produce in you? (*For instance: regret, sorrow, sadness*)

_____

_____

_____

_____

_____

4.   Reflect on God's promise of forgiveness and cleansing (1 John 1:9). Write a prayer, confessing your wrong actions to God. Make sure this prayer "agrees with God" that these actions, words, non-actions are sin. Then express this prayer to God.

(For instance: "*God, I was wrong to yell at Susie about leaving her skates in the driveway. I know I embarrassed her in front of her friend Jane. I took my frustration about the rotten day I'd had out on her, and that was wrong. Will you forgive me?*" or

"*God, I was wrong to make fun of Ashley and to bring up the driving incident in front of her friends. She must have been hurt and embarrassed. I regret how my unforgiveness has hurt her. Will you forgive me?*")

_____

_____

_____

_____

_____

5. Receive God's forgiveness and cleansing. Write a prayer of gratefulness and then express your gratefulness to God.

(For instance: "*Father, thank you that You promise in Your Word to forgive us and cleanse us when we confess our sins to you. Thank you that you forgive me when I sin. I am so grateful that you are not a God who 'keeps score' and holds grudges. Thank you that I can turn to you for forgiveness and for wisdom in how to be more intimate with my children.*")

_____

_____

_____

_____

_____

6. Empathize with your child's possible feelings. As a result of the things you've confessed to God above, what feelings might your child have experienced?

My child might have felt / did feel . . .

_____

_____

_____

_____

For example: (hurt, alone, rejected, disappointed, angry, unworthy, sad, disrespected, etc.)

7. What do you feel for your child? As you consider your child's emotions, what feelings for your child do you find stirring within you?

(For example, sadness, regret, remorse, hurt) *As I consider how I have hurt my son / daughter, I feel* _____ _____ *for him / her.*

8. Then meet with each child to confess, comfort, request forgiveness, and pray for healing (James 5:16; Matthew 5:4)

a. Express your confession(s). (#2 above)
b. Express your feelings for your child about the hurt. (#7 above)
c. Ask your child to forgive you: *Will you forgive me?* (Wait for a response.)
d. Pray for your child aloud, asking God to heal your child of all the hurt you have contributed to:

   "*Dear Lord, you know that I have hurt* _____ *through my* _____ *. Please heal him / her of all of this hurt. In Jesus Name, Amen.*

9. Close by asking your child if there are any other ways you have caused or contributed to hurt. If there are any others, take additional time to consider them and then meet again with your child, or confess it, request forgiveness, comfort, and pray for healing then. Also reassure your child that you are seeking God's help to change and grow as a parent. (Ex: *"I've told God that I know that I've been wrong. I've asked Him to help me with my anger.*)

Homework for our Homes

1. During this week, prepare a confession for each child and set aside a time to share your confession.

2. After you've shared your confession with your child, end your time with a prayer to God. Ask Him to change you in specific ways. (For instance: "*Lord, I confess to you that I was wrong to discipline Katie in anger. I'm humbled when I realize that Jesus died for my sin of inappropriate anger. Thank you that I am forgiven based not on anything I've done but on Jesus' death on the cross. Katie is so precious to me, Lord. I know she felt embarrassed and sad when I yelled at her. And I know it saddens you when she is sad. My heart's desire is that my words will build Katie up, not tear her down. Too often, though, I allow my temper to get the best of me. Often it has nothing to do with Katie but I just take it out on her. Please help me to think before I speak and demonstrate to Katie through my words and actions how much I love her. Thank you, Lord, that I can trust You to work in me to make me the father (mother) you want me to be. In Jesus' name...Amen.*")

This type of prayer models a humble and contrite heart as personal accountability is assumed. Our prayer:

◆ Affirms to the child their special sense of value and worth...that they are "worth" our apology.
◆ Challenges us as parents to fulfill our role as "living epistles."
◆ Testifies of a caring Heavenly Father who desires their best and who is saddened by their pain.

Chapter 8

———— ■ ————

LETTING YOUR CHILD KNOW YOU

(KNOWING HOW MUCH TO SAY AND WHEN TO SAY IT)

As we embarked on our journey of parenting with intimacy, we encouraged you to see your child as a gift from God—one to be unwrapped, appreciated, and treasured. We're now about to head down a slightly different, albeit parallel, road.

Have you ever considered that you are God's gift to your child? Chances are good that you've never heard such affirmation slip from your child's lips, but it's true nonetheless. Just as surely as God has entrusted your child to you as a gift to be nurtured and guided, He has given you to your child as a gift. You were hand-chosen by God to love and guide this precious child through the twists and turns of life. Just as your child is a gift that must be unwrapped, your life is a gift that must be

> Parenting with intimacy involves being real before our kids.

unwrapped and revealed to your child. Our willingness to vulnerably and appropriately disclose our lives to our children is perhaps one of the greatest gifts we can give.

We are disclosing a lot about ourselves and our marriages whether we realize it or not. II Corinthians 3:3 says we are living epistles, being known and read by all men. Our children are reading our actions, priorities, attitudes, and convictions. Our children can often feel our emotions, our moods, and even our pain. We can walk into a room having successfully conned our co-workers, the checker at the grocery store, our friends at church, perhaps even our pastor into believing that we're doing "fine...great...never better," but our children can almost always sense how we really are.. We can stay busy, do our household chores, and go about "business as usual," but our children know where our heart is. So, rather than playing games, parenting with intimacy involves being real before our kids. That's what true intimacy is all about, and it's what teaches children to be real people in a world that screams at them to live life behind a mask and to avoid what truly satisfies—intimate relationships.

Three Words for Intimacy

There are three different Hebrew words which are often translated "intimacy" in the Old Testament. The first is *"yada,"* which means to know intimately and deeply. In Psalm 139:1 David praises God for knowing him! Job also used this word when he made reference to the fact that even his *intimate* friends had betrayed him—those who knew him deeply (Job 19:14). Parenting with intimacy means knowing our children deeply just as God knows us as His children!

The second Old Testament word is "*sod*" which means to reveal, to disclose oneself. Proverbs 3:32 says that God is intimate with the upright, that is He reveals Himself to the upright. So, first He knows us (*yada*), and then He allows us to know Him (*sod*). This is part of what was going on in the Upper Room in John 15:15 when Jesus looked at His disciples one day and said, *"No longer do I call you slaves; for the slave does not know what his master is doing; but I have called you friends, for all things that I have heard from My Father I have made known to you."* It's the beauty of the Incarnation—He became flesh and dwelt among us, and we beheld Him...full of grace and truth. Part of parenting with intimacy is dwelling with your children vulnerably and transparently, allowing them to really know you, warts and all.

The third Hebrew word for intimacy is *"sakan."* David uses this word when he praises God for being intimately acquainted with all of his ways (Psalm 139:3). This word means to be caringly involved. This addresses the issue of, "Why does God want to know you? What is His motive?" Is it to judge you? criticize you? condemn you? Far from it! He wants to be intimately acquainted with you, to know you deeply, so that He can be caringly involved in your life. And this must be the motive behind our wanting to know our children - to become caringly involved in their lives.

Three beautiful dimensions of intimacy...

yada...to know

sod...to let another know you

sakan...in order to experience mutual caring involvement

These three words serve as a challenge to move us beyond passive disclosure of our lives to our children to active, purposeful disclosure. Parents, your kids need you to be more than just leaders; they need mentors and partners. They need more than just someone to point them in the right direction; they need someone to come alongside, share "war stories" about their own journey, and walk with them. Parental self-disclosure ministers to a child's sense of aloneness and fear as they hurdle each developmental milestone on their way to maturity. It encourages and empowers their progress, propelling them through difficult times. As children navigate the sometimes tumultuous and treacherous waters of growth and maturity, their parents' vulnerable self-disclosure serves as an anchor to keep them from capsizing.

STOP AND CONSIDER

Consider for a moment some "self-disclosures" from the Scriptures and then note how they might bring comfort and strength. How might these disclosures from Scripture help remove your "aloneness?"

"In the world you have tribulation, but take courage; I have overcome the world" (John 16:33).

This passage can help me not be alone when_____

_____

_____

"All authority has been given to Me in heaven and on earth...Lo, I am with you always even to the end of the age" (Matthew 28:18,20).

This passage can help me not be alone when_____

_____

_____

"Peace I leave with you; My peace I give to you; not as the world gives, do I give to you. Let not your heart be troubled, nor let it be fearful" (John 15:27).

This passage can help me not be alone when_____

_____

_____

When our aloneness is removed through vulnerable disclosure, we are blessed in many ways:

First, our *experience* is validated as real, significant, and purposeful.

Second, *hope* is engendered that someone else has already traveled this way.

Third, *trust* is deepened as vulnerable sharing allows intimates to "know" and "be known" by one another.

Finally, my *worth* is affirmed as I consider that I'm being valued as a companion and loved as a friend.

Consider now your children and these possible blessings. Who could benefit from *validation* of their experiences? *Hope* instead of fear? Deepened *trust* in relationships? An affirmation of their *worth*? Write your thoughts here:

_____

_____

A Word of Caution and Encouragement!

As you vulnerably and appropriately share yourself with your child, it is very likely that some of your own pain—both childhood and adult—may resurface. If this happens, don't deny your pain, but don't ask your child to carry your pain. If you find yourself needing someone to process this pain, find a journeymate other than your child—your spouse, a friend, a counselor, a pastor, or support group. It's important for you to have someone to share with, but your goal in disclosing yourself to your children is not to weigh them down with your own pain but to remove their aloneness.

Parents are often hesitant to disclose themselves for a number of reasons. Perhaps the strongest reason is that they're not sure what or how much to share because they may have felt all alone themselves at these developmental stages. Their own parents built walls around their lives which separated themselves emotionally from their children. Commit yourself to removing walls and tearing down fences. Let's begin our "disclosure journey."

When—And How Much— Should I Share?

Just as growing up follows a predictable developmental progression, so does parental self-disclosure. The following chart provides a summary of key intimacy disclosures across the developmental stages. Remember, it's the parents' intimacy disclosures at each developmental stage that helps a child grow and mature into the fullness of his God-intended potential.

Intimacy Disclosures

Letting Your Child Know You

In this section, we'll review the key developmental issues facing the child, and then we'll look at the important aspects of parental disclosure for each stage. (For further details about developmental stages, refer back to Chapter 3.)

Infancy (0-18 months)

As soon as baby makes his or her grand entrance into the world of bright lights and beeping delivery room monitors, he or she begins testing the waters to see if the world is a safe place. Looking for an answer to the fundamental question, *"Can relationships be trusted?"* baby sizes up the situation based on whether or not intimacy needs are met.

Parental self-disclosure at this crucial beginning stage should revolve around communicating the following and so meeting these crucial relational needs:

◆ *"We accept you into our family. You belong!"* [Acceptance]
◆ *"We're going to pay attention to your needs because we love you. You're important to us."* [Attention/Care]
◆ *"You bring joy to our lives. We're so glad God gave you to us!"* [Approval]

You may be asking yourself, "Well, how do I disclose myself to a baby who can't even talk yet?"

Don't sell baby short! From his first waking moment, baby is making assessments about the world based primarily on his interactions with you. Our best line of communication is through *tactile/sensory stimulation.* Our God-given five senses will enable us to connect with our babies as they begin to discover who we are and how important we are to them.

Touch

You speak volumes to your baby about who you are and what he means to you by the quality of your touch. Is it tender and comforting or stiff and forced? Your gentle touches tell your child she is loved and cherished. Stroking her cheek when she's contented and holding her closely when she's upset says, "I love you just like you are. I accept you as an important part of our family."

Baby is also learning that Mommy and Daddy are different. "Mommy's hands are soft. She's gentle when she pats my back and strokes my face. Daddy's hands are big and not as smooth as Mommy's. I feel safe when he holds me. When Mommy puts her cheek against mine, her face feels smooth. Daddy has whiskers; it tickles!"

Hearing

"Mommy and Daddy are different. Mommy's voice is high; Daddy's voice is deep. Mommy talks to me all day long—about everything. Daddy talks to me too, but he also makes lots of funny noises." Though his vocabulary is limited, baby senses the meaning of your words by the quality of the sound of your

> Our best line of communication is through *tactile/sensory stimulation.* Our God-given five senses will enable us to connect with our babies as they begin to discover who we are and how important we are to them.

voice. Laughter communicates joy and acceptance. Do you speak words of delight and affirmation or disgust and exasperation? Do you speak with animated inflection or in dull, wearied monotones? Do your words convey gentleness or harshness and frustration? It's not too early to heed the advice found in Proverbs 15:1, *"A gentle answer turns away wrath, but a harsh word stirs up anger."*

Smell

Let baby be with you in the kitchen (obviously in a secure place away from any potential harm). As you prepare meals, baby will enjoy discovering new smells and will begin to identify this as a place where many family's needs are met. Let baby enjoy the smell of clean laundry and the fragrance of fresh-cut flowers. Prop baby up in an infant seat or walker so he can watch you work in the yard or in the garage. He'll begin to equate certain smells with Daddy and others with Mommy. He'll also sense your acceptance and joy as he feels included into Mom and Dad's world. Again, baby will notice that Mommy and Daddy are different. "Mommy smells sweet—like baby powder lots of times! Daddy smells like Old Spice—and sometimes like sweat!"

Taste

At age-appropriate intervals, let baby begin to experiment with new tastes. "Mommy feeds me when I'm hungry. Daddy does too sometimes. Sometimes he lets me taste different things. It tastes good! And it feels good that they must love me so much because they take such good care of me."

Sight

Provide a variety of colors, shapes and designs for baby to enjoy. Trips to the grocery store provide shelf after shelf of bright-colored boxes and friendly faces. Riding on Daddy's shoulders gives baby an opportunity to view the world from a new vantage point. "Wow, Daddy's really tall!" Stroller rides and outings in the park provide a plethora of new discoveries for baby's eyes to enjoy.

There's an expression, "Mother's eyes are baby's skies." Spending many of his waking moments with you, Mom, baby watches how you interact with people and how you respond to situations. Baby is learning much from you about whether the world is a safe place. When a strange dog barks at baby on an afternoon outing in the stroller, do you yell at the dog and panic? Or, do you get down on baby's level, smile at him, and reassure him that everything is fine?

No matter what the environment you can communicate your acceptance, care and joy by your smile, laughter, and eye contact. If you watch closely your young child will focus much longer on your smiling face than on any toy or inanimate object. Even with her undeveloped sense of sight, she loves to see her mother's eyes and daddy's grin. Just smile - and share yourself with your child!

Apply the principles

No matter what your child's age, they can benefit from your self-disclosure as you meet three significant needs: acceptance, attention, and approval. How can you communicate your acceptance, attention, and approval to your infant or toddler or even older children? How might you appeal to their five senses? Make a plan for self-disclosure for each child:

Child's Name _____ I will share . . .

(For example: "*I'll share with Joey through his sense of touch. I'll initiate more tickle sessions and back rubs. That will communicate my love for him.*" "*I'll appeal to Megan's sense of smell. I'll fix her favorite hamburgers this weekend. She'll experience my joyful approval of her and my delight in her.*"

Child's Name _____

I will share _____

_____

_____

Child's Name _____

I will share _____

_____

_____

Early Childhood (18-36 months)

As a child begins the task of learning to balance the teeter-totter of *autonomy and dependency* while also resolving the issue of splitting (i.e., the Mommy/Daddy that loves me is the same Mommy/Daddy who sometimes has to tell me "no" or discipline me when I do things I shouldn't), it's important for your words as well as actions to model unconditional love. Parental self-disclosure should center around meeting specific needs through communicating:

Approval

Celebrate every little milestone in your child's journey. Birthdays, special occasions, and "no occasions" are great times to communicate in words and actions, "I'm glad you're in our family. You're special!" This conveys your approval of the way God has made him. It is absolutely essential as they begin the process of separation and individuation that they feel your support of who they are, not just what they do. As you and your child experience the inevitable power struggles of this stage, he needs you to share your positive feelings for him. "You are my beloved son (daughter) in whom I am well pleased."

Empathy/Comfort

When you sense your child is sad, disappointed, or hurt, resist giving advice, lectures, or pep talks. Share empathetic comfort from your heart: "I'm sad that you're hurting because I love you." As your child begins to experience the painful reality of not being able to always "get his way" or the startling realization that Mom can tell me "no" and still love me, she'll need the anchor of understanding. She needs parents who will share their understanding of a toddler's world. This is also a powerful ingredient in softening a child's heart to a God who cares!

Another integral part of helping your child develop empathy will be helping them understand that others have thoughts and feelings that are different. "Halley feels sad when you don't share your toys with her. I feel sad for her." "I know you feel angry at your brother right now for not taking you outside to play, but he wants to spend time with his friends right now. I'm sorry you're upset. I can remember times when I was upset with my big brother too."

Security

Begin laying the groundwork for your child's understanding that the rules and consequences you have for her are for her benefit and protection—not to cheat her out of having fun. They are an expression of your love for her. You are disclosing your great concern for her security through caring about her safety and well-being. While accepting her need for independence, you are highlighting the continued need for dependence at this stage.

At this age, "teachable moments" frequently present themselves when your child is reaping a painful consequence from disobedience of some kind. When your self-disclosure is clothed in a blanket of comfort, it will fall on a far more receptive heart. Take, for example, a toddler who has just burned her finger on a hot stove. Consider these two responses and what they disclose to the child.

"I told you not to touch the stove! That wouldn't have happened if you had obeyed me. Go in your room and stay there until it's time for dinner!"

Or, first bending down to get on her level, you kiss the hurt and then say, "I'm sorry you burned your finger. I know how much that hurts. Let's run some cold water on it to make it feel better. You know, Sweetie, when Daddy and I tell you not to do something, it's because we love you and want what's best for you."

The disclosure of your faith powerfully contributes to meeting your children's need for security. It's important at this age for your child to see that you are looking to someone outside yourself—to God—to help you. As you pray with your children at bedtime, let them hear you not only asking God to watch over them and to accomplish things in their lives but also seeking God's wisdom, presence, and provision for your life. Role model that adults, not just kids, need God!. Let your life speak of your gratefulness to Him for who He is, what He has provided, and your confidence that He will do what's in the best interest of you and your children.

Apply the principles

Consider the areas of disclosure listed above. If you have a toddler in your home, these are the priorities for self-disclosure; but every member of the family, regardless of their age, could benefit from such self-disclosures. Within the entire family, who needs your approval? your comfort? Who needs more security through your disclosures of your faith? your loving protection?

(Ex: "*Jeremy would benefit most from hearing about my faith. He's been discouraged about friendships. I want to share my faith in God's provision.*" Or "*Elizabeth would benefit most from comfort right now. She needs to hear my words of comfort about her tough soccer season.*")

Child's Name _____
     *would benefit from my disclosure of*_____

_____
_____
_____
_____

Child's Name _____
     *would benefit from my disclosure of*_____

_____
_____
_____
_____

Child's Name _____
     *would benefit from my disclosure of*_____

_____
_____
_____
_____

Early Childhood (3-5 years)

As children take *initiative* to explore the world in earnest, making daily discoveries about who they are physically, cognitively, emotionally, and sexually, parental self-disclosure focuses on three key areas:

Appreciation

Affirm your children's positive behaviors especially as they reflect character qualities. *"You do such a good job of helping me when I need it.. Thank you so much for your positive, helpful, giving attitude!"* Share with them the specific character traits you admire about them and help them see their value and benefit to others. "I'm proud of you for being such a caring friend to Jimmy." These words of appreciation help an exploring child discover his character strengths and give him the courage to tackle the world around him. (See the 30 Character Qualities in Chapter 5.)

Confession

Model a willingness to admit mistakes and ask forgiveness. "It was wrong of me not to keep my promise. Will you forgive me? As children make discoveries about themselves and the world, they must have the security of knowing mistakes are allowed. We want them to sense an environment of acceptance and forgiveness. Parents who are willing to vulnerably confess their own mistakes provide fertile soil for their child's continued growth.

One afternoon David disciplined Robin in anger for how she had talked to her mother but painfully the discipline was in anger. Leaving Robin in her room crying, David went downstairs to drink a glass of iced tea and read the paper. As God began convicting him, he began to rationalize. "Well, it wouldn't have happened if she... I'm the dad; she's the kid..." His arguments falling short, he put down his tea and went upstairs to apologize. Getting down on her level so he wouldn't tower above her, he confessed to her that he was wrong to have disciplined her in anger and asked for her forgiveness.

Remembrance

As parents share positive memories of their early years, a child's sense of identity is enhanced, especially with the same-sex parent. "I remember when I turned four. Your grandmother gave me a Lone Ranger birthday party..." "When I was five, my favorite T.V. show was..." [As an aside, this is an essential precursor to establishing same-sex peer relationships later. Through these disclosures, a young boy learns what little boys' friendships look like. He might hear about playing soccer out under the street light or camping out in the back yard. A girl learns through her mother's disclosures what girls' friendships look like. She might hear about slumber parties or playing dress up.] It's critical at this age for a child to get an initial comprehension that their parents were once that age, and that someday they'll be adults too.

Apply the principles

As you reflect on these self-disclosures...How might you share your appreciation? your confession? your remembrances? Your young child needs you to share these things about yourself, as well as the earlier stages' disclosures. But even older children can benefit from your sharing. Think about each child's world and your relationship with them. Then complete this exercise. (Ex: *"Taylor could benefit from my confession. I really lost my temper with her in McDonald's last week."* Or *"Josh could really benefit from my sharing positive memories. I've missed spending time with him these last weeks. I'll tell him fun stories about my early years. We can have great male bonding!"*)

Child's Name _____

    *would benefit from my disclosure of*_____

_____

Child's Name _____

    *would benefit from my disclosure of*_____

_____

Child's Name _____

    *would benefit from my disclosure of*_____

_____

Middle and Late Childhood
(6-11 years)

During these years your child is continuing to make discoveries about who he is and experiencing the *motivation* that comes from God's love for him. This child is able to take initiative in the challenges of grade school when she senses the firm foundation of love from those around her. Faced with such weighty issues as sibling rivalry, competition, "fairness versus justice," and his need to feel successful in the eyes of parents, peers, and other adults, it's clear that parental self-disclosure will play a pivotal role in helping stay the course as particular focus is given to:

Dreams/Aspirations

Share your own dreams and aspirations when you were at this age. Did you want to be a professional baseball player? A jet pilot? A fireman? A movie star? A fashion designer? A beautician? A doctor? Challenge your child to view the possibilities as limitless and assure him of your support and encouragement. Dream with him. Now is not the time for cold realities and practicality. Don't be a "dream-killer." Encouraging dreams will stimulate the vision God has planned for each life (Proverbs 29:18).

Decision-Making

It's tragic that so many children enter their teenage years with no experience under their belt in making decisions. Their decisions—some good and some not so good—serve as "teachable moments" to help them learn to link consequences with choices—positive and negative. Parents should share their own experiences with decision making. "I remember when I chose to _____ and experienced _____ (pain). Or, I remember when I made a wise choice to _____ and _____" (blessing). Sharing decision-making skills and some of your own positive/negative choices with your children helps remove their "aloneness" and anxiety. Allowing them to make some decisions for themselves facilitates their growing sense of identity and responsibility, as they learn to *"give an account of themselves to God"* (Romans 14:12).

Share Struggles & Resulting Success/Failure

A child this age often perceives his or her parents as always successful, invincible! Disclosing times when you've struggled, experienced failures, and experienced God's supportive love tells the child that it's possible to have those feelings and still grow up and have a meaningful life. It doesn't have to be the end of the world! "I remember how disappointed I was when I didn't _____" (Ex: make the team, pass English, get selected cheerleader, succeed at...). Help him understand that experiencing failures is not the same as being a failure and that he could *never* be a failure to you or God. Sharing the testimony of your personal salvation experience will help put life into its eternal perspective. It's important for him to be challenged with life's eternal perspective and find the deep security of God's love before he reaches the storms of adolescence.

Hope

With the doom and gloom that bombard children on a daily basis in the media, it's important for them to have hope. Share times in your life when things looked bleak and dismal but God met your need and caused *"things to work out for your good"* (Romans 8:28). Let's look at another "Adventure in Parenting" illustration from the Ferguson clan to illustrate this sharing of hope:

The Case of the Now-You-See-It-Now-You-Don't Bike. In their family devotional times, the Ferguson clan had been talking about the sovereignty of God in the life of Joseph. No matter what happened to him, Joseph saw an event as coming from God and believed God would bring forth good from it. Joseph practiced hope!

For Christmas, Eric received his first "trick" bicycle—the kind that can do all kinds of "wheelies" and jump curbs. He was so excited! One afternoon after school, Eric went to the garage to take a spin on his new bike and...it was gone! Someone had stolen it. Eric had waited so long for that bike! To say he was sad would be a gross understatement. As he and David stood together, Eric looked out over the foothills and said, "Dad, I wonder how God's going to bring good out of this!"

Well, here's what God did. Eric's grandmother heard about it and gave him $50. The homeowner's insurance paid for the stolen bike. The bicycle shop heard about it, felt sorry for Eric, and sold him a replacement bike at cost. So, Eric got a better bike and $75 to spare and experienced God as One who gives exceedingly abundant above what we could ask or think!

Eric carried that experience of hope with him into his teenage years. He was about to go to senior high and didn't have a car. As August approached, he began to fret about his transportation options. Would Mom take me? Will I have to ride the bus? Then he called on his bicycle faith and decided not to panic. God would provide...and provide He did. Eric ended up with a multicolored, customized truck the Friday before school started. Eric had learned to depend on God to meet his needs. Sometimes God might involve parents in His plan, but it was really God meeting his needs.

What was important to you at their ages

Share the things you did at this age that were uniquely you—hobbies, sports, etc. "I was really into skateboarding!" Affirm your child in areas where he is different from you as well as areas in which you're similar. "You're really good at fixing things that break; much better than I'll ever be!" It's important for him to realize that his identity is more than just being your child.

Same-Sex Friendships

By sharing experiences of same-sex friendships—memories from the past, best friends and what you did together—you encourage the same in your child. *"Uncle Stanley and I used to ride bicycles in the snow." "When I was your age, I had a best girlfriend named Linda. We did everything together."*

This further facilitates identity, separation and individuation, and healthy opposite-sex friendships later. Looking at school pictures and old yearbooks together can be a fun way to share these days of yesteryear.

The Value of Delayed Gratification

Is it any wonder that children who have known a life of one-minute oatmeal, five-minute rice, and instant pudding—not to mention having information at their fingertips within minutes on the Internet—have difficulty with delayed gratification? We as parents, of course, want to give our children "every advantage." And, yet, it is important for them to learn that sometimes, important things take time. Neglecting to do so sets them up for a rude awakening when they're out on their own and things don't come quite so easily. Sharing some of your "blessings from waiting" helps illustrate the principle: "I remember saving from my allowance for six months to help buy my first bicycle." "It took three years of trying before I finally made the team."

Paul and Vicky were, well, let's just say "older," when they married. Having waited until Paul finished his medical training, they had a few years under their belts. It was several more years before the Lord blessed them with Matthew. So, by the time Matthew arrived, Paul was established in his career and they were comfortably settled in their first house. Their experience parallels many in today's society, as many are waiting until their late-twenties and early-thirties to marry and begin a family.

They don't need to hear lectures about, "When I was a child..." They've heard it! They know how you walked barefoot to school in three feet of snow—uphill—both ways! Instead, take advantage of some "family togetherness" times to journey back with your children to days both before and since their birth when things were different for your family. These can be great times of family fun. Let's join the Ferguson clan for another trip down Memory Lane...

The Ferguson "Home Tour." David and Teresa piled Terri, Robin, and Eric in the car, and they set out on a tour of all the homes they had lived in while in Austin. At each house, they talked about what was going on with the family at that point in their lives. This provided an excellent opportunity for a discussion of successes and failures (actually, opportunities to experience growth!). Some houses represented bottom-line economic survival. Others represented sacrifices made in order for

David to finish school. "Remember when we lived here? That's when Dad was finishing his degree in nuclear physics. Einstein was his hero then. Remember that huge poster he had of Einstein hanging in the stairway?...Remember these apartments?...These are the ones Mom managed...This is the house where we had a swimming pool for the first time." At the end of their tour of homes, the Fergusons had spent time enjoyed being together, reflecting on God's faithfulness, and being reminded that life is a series of trade-offs—ups and downs—and often requires waiting, which is difficult for all of us!

Apply the principles

Your 6 to 11 year old child can benefit from these and other disclosures from prior stages. She will need your sharing of dreams, decision-making, hope, and experiences of delayed gratification. She will be encouraged to know about your early struggles and what was important to you. With all family members, how might you communicate each self-disclosure?

(Ex: "*Brad could benefit from my sharing of dreams. I want him to know that I dreamt of becoming a teacher, and yet even as that goal was achieved God also changed my dreams along the way. As Brad approaches college, I want to encourage him to dream, to reach goals, but to know that he doesn't have to settle on a dream he'll stick with forever. He and God may dream lots of different dreams!*" Or "*Jenny could benefit from my sharing about delayed gratification. She really wants to do well in the school fund raiser. I think my experience in grade school will give her encouragement.*")

Child's Name _____

    *would benefit from my disclosure of*_____

_____

Child's Name _____

    *would benefit from my disclosure of*_____

_____

Child's Name _____

    *would benefit from my disclosure of*_____

_____

Adolescence (13-18 years)

These years are ones of tremendous change. In early adolescence their thoughts, feelings, and bodies are changing so fast they can hardly keep up with them, which at least partially explains their incredible disorganization and frequents bouts of aphasia (Aphasia is a fancy name for the adolescent's tendency to "clam up", not say much, or give those famous one word responses.). In later adolescence, they begin sorting through issues of sexuality and moving from depending on their peer group as a group to developing deeper one-on-one relationships. Separation and individuation are major forces as they move toward adulthood. These kids need parents and other adults who will be committed to genuineness and integrity, qualities that will equip them to face the future with confidence, secure in their *identity* as recipients of divine love. Parental self-disclosure should focus on:

Negative/Painful Feelings

It is imperative that your teenager begin to realize that his behavior affects and influences others. One of the best ways to accomplish this is for the parent-child relationship to begin connecting on a deeper emotional level. As you, the parent, are willing to share painful feelings, your teenager begins to see the impact of his words and actions. The Holy Spirit then has the opportunity to bring conviction and repentance (John 16:8; 2 Cor. 7:10).

Eric had a habit of throwing his clothes on the floor, even the clean ones. For years Teresa had been telling him, "I get so upset when you throw your clothes on the floor. When are you going to become more responsible? Her focus had been on his behavior. On one occasion she took a slightly different angle, sharing her true feelings. "I don't know if I've ever told you this, Eric, but when I go to your closet and see clean clothes on the floor, I feel so unappreciated and taken for granted." She was not judgmental but shared her own feelings of pain. Her need to be appreciated had not been met. It was the first time it had dawned on Eric that his behaviors had the potential of positively or negatively impacting people he cared about. Up until then, he only thought, "Why is she in my room anyway?" Sharing at this level in a relationship avoids a power struggle. It's disarming...penetrating to the heart of the issue. Do I care about this person I've hurt? Eric was being called upon to practice empathy and true confession; and, over time, his behavior began to change. He was being challenged to experience Philippians 2:3—learning to think more highly of another than he would of himself—a critical issue in preparing somewhat self-centered adolescents to be more sensitive and caring in the adult world they're about to enter.

Parents often cover up their negative remembrances about their own teenage years by criticizing and nagging their kids instead. They're constantly on them because they're not bringing home all A's and B's. "You'll never make it to college. You'll never be able to get a decent job." Kids begin to tune that out. Instead, share honestly about your own feelings, particularly when there's not a current issue of conflict present. "I wish I had worked harder because my grades really hurt me when I tried to get into the college I wanted to attend. Oh, I survived; but there were consequences for my negative choices. As a result..."

Temptations

At the right time and with appropriate discretion, share with your teenager times when you were tempted...times you "passed" and times you didn't. ("I know when I said 'no' to _____ I was _____." "I remember when I compromised my convictions concerning _____, I _____." Sharing such memories strengthens their individuality and need for God and provides comfort as you minister to their aloneness. It's best to offer these disclosure when they're not struggling with that particular temptation. Otherwise, it comes across sounding like a "lecture." Family Nights would provide an appropriate time for such dialogue. Offer some biblical examples of people who confronted temptations and discuss what can be learned from their experiences (Ex: Joseph, David, Job).

Dating/Romance (Opposite-Sex Friendships)

Share memories of your first date and first girlfriend/boyfriend. This not only begins to reassure them that Mom and Dad were really normal teenagers themselves, but also lets them see that the first person they date may or may not be the person they end up marrying. Sharing some of the awkward and funny dating lessons helps teens better deal with their own inadequacies and insecurities. This can be liberating.

Parental Inadequacies/Admiration of Child's Gifts

Be willing to vulnerably share your own inadequacies and how you deal with them. At the same time, identify areas that your child is better at than you are, and affirm them. "Terri, you're really a creative decorator; we may get you to redo our whole house!" "Robin, you're so organized and responsible; I think we'll let you run our life!" "Eric, I wish I had the mechanical ability you have; we're going to hire you as our resident handyman." This will reinforce the legitimacy of your child's individuality and communicate that they are free to be their own person. It also models for them that they can be happy for a friend's achievements and abilities that exceed their own. This is hard for all of us to master. What better time to lay the groundwork.

Apply the principles

Teenagers can certainly benefit from these disclosures. They'll need someone to come alongside and walk arm-in-arm through these sometimes turbulent years. But don't forget about the earlier self-disclosures. At times, your teen may need to hear those as well. Which family member could benefit from each disclosure?

(Ex: "*Michael could benefit from my sharing of painful feelings. When he demands instant response about his concerns, I feel taken advantage of—taken for granted. Sharing my feelings may help remind him to consider others' feelings and needs.*" Or "*Shannon could benefit from my sharing about dating relationships. She could benefit from both a male and female perspective on how to interact on a date, refuse a date, and say "good night."*")

Child's Name _____
    would benefit from my disclosure of_____
_____
_____
_____
_____

Child's Name _____
    would benefit from my disclosure of_____
_____
_____
_____
_____

Child's Name _____
    would benefit from my disclosure of_____
_____
_____
_____
_____

Young Adult (19-30 years)

Your relationship with your child is entering a new phase. Now you are fellow adults. Although this is what you've been preparing them for, it's often difficult for parents to face. It's only natural to grieve somewhat over things that will never be again, but embrace the new depth and breadth of communication that awaits you. As they leave home for school, careers, and marriage, your times of one-on-one dialogue will diminish, so make the most of the opportunities when they arise. Parental self-disclosure should revolve around the following:

Enjoyment of Common Interests

Acknowledge your recognition that you are now fellow adults and that, while you will always be available for imparting parental wisdom and counsel when he chooses to seek it, you also look forward to expanding your relationship into new dimensions. "It's such a blessing just to enjoy our friendship together." Common interests that you develop together will become a testimony and reminder of your new adult-to-adult relationship. "I'm looking forward to us exploring some fun common interests."

Painful Remembrances/Regrets

Share with your young adult things you wish you had done differently and why. "I deeply regret not being more involved in your school activities as you were growing up." This is a courageous move because all parents, for the most part, do the best they can; but we realize along the way that even though our motives were good, our methods may have been hurtful. "Thinking I was 'providing' for the family, I worked many more hours than I wish I had; I missed being with you more and I regret it." This demonstration of your commitment to truth will open doors of communication that might otherwise have remained shut and impeded your child's ability to develop vulnerable, intimate relationships with others.

Confession

The next step is to develop a whole new dimension of confession. After you've shared the areas you're aware of that are in need of confession and forgiveness, then acknowledge to your young adult that you realize there are surely others you're not aware of. Give them permission to share those in love, genuinely asking them to reveal to you areas where you may have unknowingly hurt them. "I know there have been times when I've disappointed you or let you down, and not even realized it. As the Lord brings them to your heart, I'd really like for you to share them so we can visit about them and heal them. I want to hear them because I love you." This is a vulnerable, selfless move, calling for a servant's heart willing to go beyond the natural desire to defend oneself to responding compassionately and repentantly in order to achieve a higher good.

David "dated" Terri and Robin from the time they were twelve. On these father-daughter outings he helped them with their chair, opened doors for them, helped them with their coats, brought them little gifts...role-modeling for them how they should expect the young men in their lives to treat them. When Terri was about nineteen and a student at the University of Texas, she and David were on a lunch date when he opened up this door of self-disclosure.

"Terri, I know there have been times when I've disappointed you or let you down. I wonder if there are any that we haven't talked about that might be on your heart. If there are, I'd really like to talk about them."

Of course, he was hoping she'd say, "No, Dad. Everything's fine." Instead, she said...

"Well, Dad, there is. Remember when I graduated from high school last year?"

David remembered. In fact, he scanned his memory bank, checking things off... "I showed up...I was on time...I brought a gift...We went out afterward as a family..." Things seemed to be in order.

"Dad, remember I was working part-time that semester. The rest of the family went on down to the Berger Center where the graduation was to take place. Well, this may sound strange, but, it felt funny that day to leave my job and drive myself to my own graduation. It would have meant so much to me if some-body could have come by and picked me up."

She was being vulnerable about something that had both-ered her for a year. David's response was to empathize with her. "Sweetheart, it saddens me that hurt you. I really regret what I did. I love you and care about you, and I don't want to hurt you."

"Thanks, Dad. That means a lot to me." And it's healed.

During one of our brainstorming sessions for writing this book, Robin revealed an area of hurt that dated back to her high school days as well. Although she enjoyed her thirteen years in a private Christian school, it had bothered her that she felt uninvolved in the decision-making process. It was obviously an area that needed comforting, because just sharing it brought tears to her eyes. David took the opportunity to go sit next to her, put his arm around her, and acknowledge the area of hurt and minister comfort to her.

Are you willing to make yourself vulnerable in this way? Confession produces a sense of security that invites future dia-logue and promises a deepening relationship as you relate adult-to-adult. What greater joy could any parent desire!

Need for Mutual Giving

In the early years of a child's life, the parents are primarily in the position of giving to the child. But as the child reaches adulthood, he becomes equipped for mutual giving. Young adults have matured to the point where they can now give to the needs of their parents. The challenge comes in doing this within the confines of healthy, appropriate boundaries.

At one point in his career, David's father was a building inspector. When David became involved in some real estate ven-tures, he was able to call upon one of his dad's areas of strength to tap into this need to be needed. "Dad, do you think you could inspect this property for me before I buy it? I could sure use your expertise." On an adult-to-adult level, David acknowledged his ongoing need for his father's wise counsel. His mother, on the other hand, was gifted in the area of working with numbers. So guess who became David's tax specialist for the next ten years!

Without openly addressing a parent's need to be needed, this area has great potential for misunderstanding as boundaries are perceived as been encroached upon. However, if healthy self-disclosure has been taking place at the previous developmental stages, the groundwork has been laid for open, honest communication. Parents, don't be afraid to express your needs, speaking the truth in love, while at the same time acknowledging and affirming your adult child's need to be independent. Affirm the blessing of your young adult "giving" to minister to your intimacy needs. "I really appreciated being able to help with your remodeling projects. It feels great to still be needed." "It really meant a lot to me last week when you called me, checking on the outcome of my important meeting. Thanks!"

These can be years of tremendous satisfaction and fulfillment as you watch your child spread his or her wings and fly like an eagle!

Apply the principles

What disclosures might your young adult children need to hear? Consider their worlds and your relationship with them. Who could benefit from enjoying common interests? sharing regret? confession? opportunity for mutual giving?

(Ex: Timothy could benefit from my sharing a common interest. He's been playing a lot of golf lately; perhaps that's one way we could spend more time together. I'll invite him to the driving range next week. ... Cara could benefit from my sharing my regrets about her high school years. When her dad and I separated, I turned to Cara for support. I regret burdening her with my hurts. I know she faced responsibilities that weren't hers to face. She missed out on the chance "just to be a teenager"— like that isn't hard enough!

Young Adult's Name _____
could benefit from my sharing _____
_____
_____
_____
_____

Young Adult's Name _____
could benefit from my sharing _____
_____
_____
_____
_____

Young Adult's Name _____
could benefit from my sharing _____
_____
_____
_____
_____

Scripture Journaling and Prayer - Isaiah 40:30-31

"Though youths grow weary and tired, and vigorous young men stumble badly, yet those who wait for the Lord will gain new strength; they will mount up with wings like eagles, they will run and not get tired, they will walk and not become weary."

Reflect on the Lord's promise of "new strength" at any time of life. As you have identified needed strength for yourself, your spouse, and your children, ask Him for it now. Write your thoughts below.

For myself, as spouse, parent, and Your child, I need_____

_____

_____

_____

For my spouse, I ask for_____

_____

_____

_____

For my child _____, I ask for_____

_____

_____

(For instance: *"Lord, I need Your strength to share times of confession with my children. God, my children need Your strength to withstand the temptations of peer pressure."*)

Now pause and thank Him by faith for His strength to each person, expressing your gratefulness that He attends to our needs. Write your prayer here:

_____

_____

_____

_____

_____

_____

Special Thoughts for Single Parents

Allow your kids to know about your own hurts. While considering their age and development, let them know that you hurt over the divorce or death. Express your regrets and sadness, but don't expect them to meet your emotional needs. Expressing your pain lets them hear the truth about the situation, since the uncertainty is often more frightening than reality. Reassure your kids that the divorce or death was not their fault. They did nothing wrong.

Special Thoughts for Blended Families

Tell your children about the challenges you face as parents in a blended family. Let them know that blending a family is difficult, but that you and your spouse are committed to doing the work. Verbalize your commitment to responsible parenting. It is not your children's job to work at blending a family. Relay this information with the motive of communicating truth to your children. Don't expect your children to meet your need for comfort or appreciation.

This may also be the time when you let your children know that you see divorce as wrong but forgivable. As appropriate, acknowledge your own part in hurting your child through the divorce. Set aside some private time with each child. Give specific examples of the hurts your child might have experienced. Share your regret and sadness for her pain. With humility, ask for your child's forgiveness. Then share your hope because of God's gracious plan for healing.

Experiencing Biblical Truth

Bless the Lord, O my soul,
And forget none of His benefits. Psalm 103:2

1. You have experienced all three Hebrew concepts of "intimacy" as you worked through this material. You have developed a deeper personal awareness and understanding of your spouse or partner ("yada"). What feelings does that produce in you? How does it feel to <u>know</u> your partner better today than you did before? I feel...(blessed, honored, close, connected, happy, etc.)

2. Share these feelings with your partner. Allow time for each person to share their feelings about this deeper awareness and understanding.

3. You have also experienced the concept of vulnerable disclosure ("sod") You have revealed or disclosed yourself to another person. What feelings does this produce in you? How does it feel to <u>be known</u> by your spouse or partner? I feel...(close, vulnerable, intimate, awkward, etc.)

4. Share these feelings with your partner. Allow time for each person to express how they felt about revealing himself to another person.

5. Each of you, we hope, have experienced the concept of intimacy as "caring involvement" ("sakan"). We hope you have entered into your partner's world and let them enter yours - not out of duty, obligation, or selfishness - but because you care. We hope you have invested yourself in the life of another person and allowed them to be involved with you because of a sincere motive of loving concern. If this has been true for you, we ask that you share this with your partner. Your words might sound like, *It has been my privilege to get to know you and let you get to know me today. I care about the things you've shared with me - the joys, the hurts, the fears and struggles.* Write your words here:

6. Take a few moments and reflect on your journey through this material. Reflect on the Heavenly Father's example in parenting: He has created us to need both an intimate relationship with Him and with other people. He's a parent who

initiates relationship; Our Heavenly Father created us with needs that He abundantly supplies Himself and through those around us - He's a parent who provides; Our Heavenly Father parents us with unconditional love. He's a parent who separates our worth from our behavior; Our Heavenly Father cares about each of our emotions. He rejoices when we're rejoicing. His heart breaks when we're hurting. He's the God of all comfort; And finally, our Heavenly Father not only wants to know us, He lets us know Him through the life of His Son and the testimony of His Word. He's a parent who reveals Himself. What aspect of our Heavenly Father's parenting has meant the most to you? Write your thoughts here:

I'm grateful for my Heavenly Father because . . .

_____
_____
_____
_____

(For instance: "*I'm grateful for my Heavenly Father because He never relates to me from a distance. He's always ready to receive me, listen to me, comfort me, and be with me. He's consistently loving and constantly present.*")

7. As you reflect on our Heavenly Father's example, what changes could be needed in your own parenting? How might God want to change you? Complete your thoughts below:

As I reflect on my Heavenly Father, I know God wants to make me a more _____ parent. Therefore, I am committed to . . . _____

_____
_____

(or)

_____
_____
_____

*As I reflect on my Heavenly Father, I know God wants to make me a less _____ parent. Therefore, I am committed to . . .*_____

_____

_____

_____

_____

_____

(For instance: "*As I reflect on my Heavenly Father, I know God wants to make me a more consistent parent. Therefore, I am committed to discussing parenting decisions and expectations with my spouse. I will work with my partner to set rules for our home and stick with them.*" Or "*As I reflect on my Heavenly Father, I know God wants to make me a less critical parent. Therefore, I am committed to healing my own hurt and anger so that I don't take it out on my kids. I will do this by meeting with our pastor and small group.*")

8. Share your reflects and commitments with your spouse or partner.

Homework for Our Homes

Look over the Intimacy Disclosures chart and determine which developmental stage each of your children is in. Take the time to reflect on the important disclosures for those stages. Now make a plan for those disclosures. It might be as simple as setting aside "talking time" in the car. Start your disclosures with sentences such as, "I remember the time when . . ." or "I'd like to tell you a story about the time I . . ." You might also want to write your stories in a journal for you and your child to read together. Make sure to provide illustrations or photographs if possible. And finally, you might begin family nights or meals together with disclosures about yourself. No matter what your format, remember the goal of "letting your child know you."

Appendix A

———— ◆ ————

Stop and Consider

─────────────────────────────────

STOP AND CONSIDER THE INFANCY STAGE

Stop and consider: If your child is a newborn, you might meet needs for acceptance and affection by:

1. Being consistently responsive to your child's cries.
2. Letting your child touch your nose, face and mouth while he or she is feeding.
3. Touching your child gently, caressing and stroking your child, giving a massage.
4. Using a soft tone of voice, talking to your infant in "baby talk"—they really do respond best to a high pitched tone of voice!
5. Providing changes of scenery for your infant—they love the variety of sensory experience.
6. Cuddling your child, rocking, holding, gently tickling your infant, nuzzling your head into your child's tummy, playing peek-a-boo.

Consider the ideas above. Which areas of acceptance and affection might you need to implement or increase? How might you continue to meet your infant's need for acceptance, thus fostering trust in your and God's love? Write your ideas here:

_____

_____

_____

_____

_____

If your child has passed this developmental stage, what positive memories do you have about this stage? What fond memories come to mind as you think about the demonstrations of love listed above? *I have fond memories of meeting my baby's need for acceptance through ...*_____

_____

_____

_____

_____

Do you wish you had done anything differently? More or less of anything? Write about it here: *"I wish I had . . .*

_____

_____

Spend some time expressing the above to God, asking and experiencing His forgiveness as necessary. And consider talking to your child about this as well, maybe even confessing and seeking an older child's forgiveness.

_____

STOP AND CONSIDER THE TODDLER STAGE

How well are you managing the toddler years? Showing loving acceptance during these years might look like:

1. Child-proofing your home—removing or fencing off hazards allows a child to explore their world. It communicates our acceptance of their natural curiosity and need to explore as well as meeting their need for security.
2. Being consistent with rules and limits. If it's NOT OK to jump on the couch today, it shouldn't be OK tomorrow.
3. Allowing plenty of opportunities and flexibility for your child to sit and cuddle with you one minute and get down and play the next. Accept your child's fluctuations and preferences.
4. Ignoring or giving no attention to a temper tantrum. Out in public it might mean retreating to the car, the curb or the restroom. When the storm subsides, resume your activity. (Aren't we glad that God ignores some of our tantrums?!)
5. Saying, "I love you" after a tantrum or power struggle—not "I love you now that that's over" or "I love you anyway"—just, "I love you."

Consider the ideas above. Which areas of acceptance might you need to implement or increase? How else might you continue to meet your child's need for acceptance and help him balance autonomy and dependency? Write your ideas here:

_____

_____

_____

_____

_____

If your child is past this developmental stage, what fond memories do you have of his toddler years? As you read the ideas for acceptance in this stage, what memories made you smile? *I have fond memories of showing my child acceptance when* . . ._____

_____

_____

Do you wish you had done anything differently? More or less of anything? Write about it here: *"I wish I had . . .*

_____

_____

_____

Spend some time expressing the above to God, asking and experiencing His forgiveness as necessary. And consider talking to your child about this as well, maybe even confessing and seeking your child's forgiveness.

STOP AND CONSIDER THE EARLY CHILDHOOD STAGE

Stop and consider the Early Childhood years of discovery. How are you and your child handling the rapid physical, cognitive, sexual development? Expressing unconditional loving acceptance and attention to a child this age might involve:

1. Giving plenty of time and opportunities for running, jumping, and climbing—fostering the discovery of all one's body can do.
2. Answering questions about bodies and body parts with age-appropriate facts and truthful information.
3. Answering "why" questions with patience and kindness—not with "because I said so!"
4. Providing opportunities for your child to imitate the adults around him. That might include: pushing a child-sized shopping cart or pretending to shave like Daddy.
5. Teaching your child about relationships and values through storytelling and reading books.
6. Playing with your children in their world of pretend and not worrying too much about "real life" at these times. Join in the "tea parties," the "classroom," or the "doctor's office" and let their imaginations run the show.

Consider the ideas above. **Which areas might you need to implement or increase?** How might you continue to meet your children's needs for acceptance and help them discover and develop their strengths? Write your ideas here:

_____

_____

_____

_____

If your child has passed this developmental stage, what fond memories do you have of their preschool years? What positive images come to mind when you think about the ways to show acceptance during this stage? *I have fond memories of the time I showed my preschooler accept-ance by . . .*

_____

_____

_____

_____

Do you wish you had done anything differently? More or less of any-thing? Write about it here: *"I wish I had . . .*

_____

_____

_____

_____

Spend some time expressing the above to God, asking and experienc-ing His forgiveness as necessary. And consider talking to your child about this as well, maybe even confessing and seeking your child's forgiveness.

_____

Stop and Consider the Middle and Late Childhood Stage

Stop and consider the middle and late childhood years. How are you and your grade school child managing these years? Meeting your children's needs especially for acceptance but also for attention, approval, comfort, security, encouragement and support might require:

1. Addressing any of the three "dangerous" reasons for sibling rivalry and deal with typical sibling competition with patience and limits. Allow children to work out differences between themselves as much as possible. You might intervene if property is about to be damaged, if physical harm is about to occur or if you just can't stand it any longer. Divide and conquer—send the offending siblings outside to work it out or call for a separation of space. Let go of the temptation to try and referee. It's futile to try and sort out "who did what" first. Instead: *"If you're going to continue to play, you'll need to get along with one another; if not, you'll need to stop playing together and do something separately."*

2. Involving ourselves in our child's competitive world. Be there for the games, concerts, and contests. Empathize and comfort when your child has struggles or loses in a competition, *"Honey, I know tonight was hard for you. I know you were hoping the coach would play you more. I feel sad for you."* Celebrate when your child has victories, *"Wow! What a terrific play! Your hard work really paid off. I knew you'd nail those lines."*

3. Purposefully developing relationships with families who can be a positive force in the life of your child. Develop relationships with other families whose children are of similar ages and interests—Find families whose kids enjoy video games and Science exhibits, if that's what your family is "into". Develop relationships at church with other adults who can have a positive impact on your child. Join the YMCA, Boy Scouts or children's club at church. Let your children experience the encouragement and challenge of other caring adults.

Consider the ideas above. Which areas of loving care might you need to implement or increase? How might you continue to meet your child's need especially for acceptance as well as many other needs? Write your ideas here:

_____

_____

_____

_____

   If your child has passed this developmental stage, what positive memories do you have about these years? As you read the ideas for meeting the needs, what remembrances made you smile? *I smile when I think about giving my child acceptance when . . .*

_____

_____

   Do you wish you had done **anything** differently? More or less of anything? Write about it here: *"I wish I had . . .*

_____

_____

   Spend some time expressing the above to God, asking and experiencing His forgiveness as necessary. And consider talking to your child about this as well, maybe even confessing and seeking your child's forgiveness.

_____

Stop and Consider the Early Adolescence Stage

Stop and consider the years of early adolescence (11—13 years). How are you doing at helping your young adolescent negotiate the challenges and changes that come with puberty? Acceptance of your young person might look like:

1. **Accepting your teen's reluctance to talk.** Adults have a tendency to increase the amount of their words in direct proportion to the decrease in their teen. Fewer words will most likely have the best impact on your teen. Ask open ended or conversation starting questions, "What was the best thing about your week at camp?" or "Tell me something you enjoyed doing on your vacation. I'd like to hear about it! Mix your questions with statements of observation: "You look like you might be feeling a little down. Need to talk?" Or "It sounds like you might be disappointed in your friend. Would that fit?"
2. **Providing opportunities for your adolescent to safely and appropriately spend time with the opposite sex.** Provide supervised times of group activities—where groups of boys can spend time with groups of girls. Encourage your child to attend church activities, as well as school-sponsored events, community service projects and neighborhood social gatherings. And don't forget to get involved yourself as a sponsor, chaperone, or volunteer.
3. **Being careful to pick your battles.** Consider issues of conflict carefully. Issues of conflict may be a teen's way of separating from you and becoming an individual. Your teens' separation might look like: styles of clothing that you hate, choices of hair style that you find ridiculous, or music preferences that you find distasteful. As difficult as it may seem, allow your child to have some choices in these areas. Prayerfully consider what are the "big issues" and what can you let go? You might allow your teen to choose any shirt in his closet for school but ask that he wear T-shirts without logos for church. Your teen might be allowed to buy CD's with money she earns, but you might require that she choose CD's that don't endorse violence, sex, or gang activity.

Think about the ideas above. Which areas of acceptance might you need to implement or increase? How might you continue to meet your child's need for acceptance and help him continue to grow up as God intends?

Write your ideas here:

_____

_____

_____

_____

If your child has passed this developmental stage, what positive memories do you have about these years? As you read the ideas for demonstrating acceptance, what fond memories came to mind? *I remember meeting my son/daughter's need for acceptance during the junior high years. One particular time comes to mind when . . .*

_____

_____

_____

_____

Do you wish you had done anything differently? More or less of anything? Write about it here: *"I wish I had . . .*

_____

_____

_____

_____

Spend some time expressing the above to God, asking and experiencing His forgiveness as necessary. And consider talking to your child about this as well, maybe even confessing and seeking your child's forgiveness.

Stop and Consider the Middle Adolescence Stage

How well are you dealing with these years of middle adolescence? How well are you communicating acceptance to your teenager as well as meeting other important needs? Showing acceptance to your teenager might look like:

1. Responding with patience and respect when your teen vacillates in his/her commitment to friends. This will mean being careful not to make fun of your teen or dismiss or belittle her feelings: 'Yeah, you say that now, but you'll be best friends again tomorrow." You'll want to avoid sarcasm and teasing statements such as, "Oh, so you two are best friends again?" Or "I thought you'd gotten over your little spat with Heather."
2. Being careful not to intentionally embarrass or call attention to your teen in any negative way. Remember, your teen is especially sensitive about his negative characteristics. You'll want to avoid comments about his skin, hair, clothing, personal habits or grooming in front of other people. Be careful of talking to your friends about any topic that your teen would consider sensitive or personal information. Bragging about your teen's accomplishments is acceptable, making fun of his poor driving is not. Complimenting your teen on her dress is appropriate, telling her to keep using the astringent on her skin is not.
3. Allowing your teen to discover "how smart you are" on her own terms. It will take great patience and self restraint, but limit the number of "I told you so's." Bite your lip when your son comes home and announces, "It's not fair! They won't give me my grades until I pay the library fines!" Hold your tongue when your daughter comes home in tears because someone has stolen her purse—and she forgot to lock the car. Even if you've told them a thousand times, let them learn those life lessons on their own. Give comfort, show understanding, respond with care and concern. Let go of the phrase, "If you'd only listen . . .".

Think about the ideas above. Which areas of acceptance and other giving to meet needs might you need to implement or increase?

Write your ideas here:

_____

_____

_____

_____

If your child is past this developmental stage, what positive memories do you have about these years? As you read the ideas for showing acceptance to a child this age, what memories made you smile? *I smile when I remember showing my kid acceptance. One of those times was when . . .*

_____

_____

_____

_____

Do you wish you had done anything differently? More or less of anything? Write about it here: *"I wish I had . . .*

_____

_____

_____

_____

_____

STOP AND CONSIDER THE YOUNG ADULT STAGE

Stop and consider your son's/daughter's transition years to becoming a young adult. How are the two of you negotiating the transition into full autonomy? What demonstrations of acceptance might be needed? Acceptance as well as giving to meet other needs might look like:

1. Asking if your son or daughter would like your input instead of just giving it unsolicited. Offer to give feedback and then wait for the go ahead. This might sound like, *"Your Dad and I have thought about ways we might help you get settled into your new apartment. Would that be something you'd like to discuss?"* Secondly, give your feedback and then leave it at that. This might sound like: *"I've always found Pastor Edwards to be a great source of support and wise counsel. He might be someone you could talk to about service opportunities. That's just one idea. I know you'll find the information and support you need."*
2. Taking the initiative to be with your child, just to be together, not to deal with "business." Call, write, e-mail: Hi! I was thinking about you. Just wanted to tell you I love you and I'm so grateful to have you as a son/daughter. Ask to go to breakfast or lunch.
3. Asking your son or daughter's opinion about something and then just listening and affirming their expression without criticism and without expressing your own. Then thank them for sharing theirs!
4. Providing and initiating a time of confession and forgiveness. Pray and ask God to reveal to you how you might have hurt your child. Then confess to God and receive His forgiveness (I John 1:9). Next, confess to your child (James 5:16). This might sound like, *"I know I've not been a perfect parent. There's been times I have hurt you and disap-pointed you. I'd like to hear about those times and understand how you've felt. I love you and want to heal any hurts that might be there."*

Before you start this kind of discussion, be ready to listen without defensiveness, giving justification, excuses or hostility. Listen to your child. Rephrase their words so they know you understand. Then give words of consolation and comfort. *"I'm so sad I was a part of hurting you."*

"I know that time was difficult for you. I hurt when I think about you needing security and reassurance of my love."

Think about the ideas above. Which areas of acceptance might you need to implement or increase? How might you continue to meet your son or daughter's need for acceptance and help him/her become the man God intends him to be? /become the woman God desires? Write your thoughts here:

_____
_____
_____

If your child has passed this developmental stage, what positive memories do you have about his/her young adult years? As you remember your expressions of acceptance, which memories bring a smile to your face? *I remember demonstrating acceptance to my young adult when . . .*

_____
_____
_____

Do you wish you had done anything differently? More or less of anything? Write about it here: *"I wish I had . . .*

_____
_____
_____
_____

Spend some time expressing the above to God, asking and experiencing His forgiveness as necessary. And consider talking to your child about this as well, maybe even confessing and seeking your child's forgiveness.

_____

Appendix B

——— ◆ ———

Assessing Relational Needs Questionnaire

While we all have the same relational needs, the *priority* of those needs is different for each person. Your greatest need may be for *affection*, while your partner's greatest need may be *security*. One child may have an acute need for *comfort*, but another sibling's greatest need may be *encouragement*. *Appreciation* may be at the top of the list for your next door neighbor, while your tennis buddy needs *approval* more than anything else.

An important aspect of learning to love an individual is taking the time to know them and to discover what their unique needs are. Perhaps this is what Peter meant when he admonished husbands to, *"Live with your wives in an understanding way"* (1 Peter 3:7). It may also be a part of how a woman, *"Watches over the affairs of her household"* (Proverbs 31:27). It is, no doubt, part of parents "unwrapping" the gifts that God has given them through children, *"Children are a gift from the Lord"* (Psalms 127:3).

This questionnaire will help an individual assess his or her most important relational needs. Answer the questions, then score the questionnaire to identify which needs you perceived as most important. Have family members, friends, ministry team members, etc. complete the questionnaire and then discuss the results.

Name: _____ Date Completed: _____

Instructions: Personally respond to these questions by placing the appropriate number beside each sentence. Then, use the "interpretation chart" to identify which needs you perceived as most important. Later, discuss your results with friends or journey-mates who have also completed it.

Intimacy Needs Assessment Tool

Page One

Strongly disagree	Disagree	Neutral	Agree	Strongly agree
-2	-1	0	+1	+2

_____ 1. It's important that people receive me for who I am, even if I'm a little "different."

_____ 2. It's important to me that my financial world be in order.

_____ 3. I sometimes become "weary in well doing."

_____ 4. It's vital to me that others ask me my opinion.

_____ 5. It's important that I receive physical hugs, warm embraces, etc...

_____ 6. I feel good when someone "enters into my world."

_____ 7. It's important for me to know "where I stand" with those who are in authority over me.

_____ 8. It is meaningful when someone notices that I need help and then they offer to get involved.

_____ 9. If I feel overwhelmed, I want someone to come alongside me and help.

_____ 10. I feel blessed when someone recognizes and shows concern for how I'm feeling.

_____ 11. I like to know if "who I am" is of value and is meaningful to others.

_____ 12. Generally speaking, I don't like a lot of solitude.

_____ 13. It means a lot to me for loved ones to initiate saying to me, "I love you."

_____ 14. I resist being seen only as a part of a large group—my individuality is important.

_____ 15. I am blessed when a friend calls to listen and encourage me.

_____ 16. It's important to me that people acknowledge me not just for what I do but for who I am.

_____ 17. I feel best when my world is orderly and somewhat predictable.

_____ 18. When I've worked hard on something, I am pleased when others express gratitude.

_____ 19. When I "blow it," it's important to me to be reassured that I'm still loved.

_____ 20. It's encouraging to me that others notice my effort or accomplishments.

_____ 21. I sometimes feel overwhelmed with all I have to do.

Intimacy Needs Assessment Tool

Page Two

Strongly disagree	Disagree	Neutral	Agree	Strongly agree
-2	-1	0	+1	+2

_____ 22. I want to be treated with kindness and equality by all regardless of my race, gender, looks, or status.

_____ 23. I like to be greeted with a handshake or other appropriate friendly touch.

_____ 24. I like it when someone wants to spend time with me.

_____ 25. I am blessed when a "superior" says, "Good job."

_____ 26. It's important to me for someone to express care for me after I've had a hard day.

_____ 27. When facing something difficult, I usually sense that I need other people's input and help.

_____ 28. Written notes and calls expressing sympathy after a serious loss or difficulty are (or would be) meaningful to me.

_____ 29. I feel good when someone close to me shows satisfaction with the way I am.

_____ 30. I enjoy being spoken of or mentioned in front of other people.

_____ 31. I would be described as a person who likes hugs and/or other caring touch.

_____ 32. When a decision is going to affect me, it's important to me that I am involved in the decision.

_____ 33. I am blessed when someone shows interest in what I'm working on.

_____ 34. I appreciate trophies, plaques, or special gifts as permanent reminders of something significant I have done.

_____ 35. I sometimes worry about the future.

_____ 36. When I'm introduced into a new environment, I typically search for a group to connect with.

_____ 37. The thought of change (moving, new job....etc.) produces anxiety for me.

_____ 38. It bothers me when people are prejudiced against someone just because they dress or act differently.

_____ 39. I want to be close to friends and loved ones who will be there "through thick and thin."

_____ 40. I am blessed by written notes and other specific expressions of gratitude.

Intimacy Needs Assessment Tool

Page Three

Strongly disagree	Disagree	Neutral	Agree	Strongly agree
-2	-1	0	+1	+2

_____ 41. To know that someone is praying for me is meaningful to me.

_____ 42. I am bothered by "controlling" people.

_____ 43. I am blessed when I receive unmerited and spontaneous expressions of love.

_____ 44. I am pleased when someone carefully listens to me.

_____ 45. I am blessed when people commend me for a godly characteristic I exhibit.

_____ 46. I typically don't want to be alone when experiencing hurt and trouble.

_____ 47. I don't enjoy working on a project by myself; I prefer to have a partner.

_____ 48. It's important for me to feel a "part of the group."

_____ 49. I respond to someone who tries to understand me and who shows me loving concern.

_____ 50. I would rather work with a team of people than by myself.

"Assessing Relational Needs" Questionnaire
Scoring

1. Add up your responses
(-2, -1, 0, +1, +2) to items:

    1 _____

    19 _____

    36 _____

    38 _____

    48 _____

Total _____

These responses relate to the need for ACCEPTANCE.

2. Add up your responses to items:

    2 _____

    17 _____

    35 _____

    37 _____

    39 _____

Total _____

These responses relate to the need for SECURITY

3. Add up your responses to items:

    18 _____

    20 _____

    25 _____

    34 _____

    40 _____

Total _____

These responses relate to the need for APPRECIATION

4. Add up your responses to items:

    3 _____

    15 _____

    21 _____

    33 _____

    41 _____

Total _____

These responses relate to the need for ENCOURAGEMENT

5. Add up your responses to items:

    4 _____

    14 _____

    22 _____

    32 _____

    42 _____

Total _____

These responses relate to the need for RESPECT.

6. Add up your responses to items:

    5 _____

    13 _____

    23 _____

    31 _____

    43 _____

Total _____

These responses relate to the need for AFFECTION.

7. Add up your responses to items:

    6 _____

    12 _____

    24 _____

    30 _____

    44 _____

Total _____

These responses relate to the need for ATTENTION.

8. Add up your responses to items:

    7 _____

    11 _____

    16 _____

    29 _____

    45 _____

Total _____

These responses relate to the need for APPROVAL

9. Add up your responses to items:

    10 _____

    26 _____

    28 _____

    46 _____

    49 _____

Total _____

These responses relate to the need for COMFORT.

10. Add up your responses to items:

    8 _____

    9 _____

    27 _____

    47 _____

    50 _____

Total _____

These responses relate to the need for SUPPORT.

For Reflection or Discussion:

1.   What were your three highest totals? Which needs do they repre-
     sent?

     • _____
     • _____
     • _____

2.   What were your three lowest totals? Which needs do they repre-
     sent?

     • _____
     • _____
     • _____

3.   If others are completing this questionnaire with you (friend,
     spouse, fiancé, other family members, ministry team members,
     etc.), what were their highest and lowest totals?

     3 Highest:
     • _____
     • _____
     • _____

     3 Lowest:
     • _____
     • _____
     • _____

4.   What might be the implications of your scores compared to their
     scores?

About the Great Commandment Network

The Great Commandment Network is an international collaborative network of strategic kingdom leaders from the faith community, marketplace, education, and caregiving fields who prioritize the powerful simplicity of the words of Jesus to love God, love others, and see others become His followers (Matthew 22:37–40; 19–20).

The Great Commandment Network is served through these entities.

Relationship Press

This team collaborates, supports, and joins together with churches, denominational partners, and professional associates to develop, print, and produce resources that facilitate ongoing Great Commandment ministry.

The Center for Relational Leadership

Their mission is to teach, train, and mentor both ministry and corporate leaders in Great Commandment principles, seeking to equip leaders with relational skills, so they might lead as Jesus led.

The Galatians 6:6 Retreat Ministry

This ministry offers a unique two-day retreat for ministers and their spouses for personal renewal and for reestablishing and affirming ministry and family priorities.

The Center for Relational Care (CRC)

The CRC provides therapy and support to relationships in crisis through an accelerated process of growth and healing, including Relational Care Intensives for couples, families, and singles.

For more information on how you, your church, ministry, denomination, or movement can be served by the Great Commandment Network write or call:

Great Commandment Network
2511 South Lakeline Blvd.
Cedar Park, Texas 78613
Phone: 800.881.8008

Visit our website at www.GreatCommandment.net